PATRICK LOSE'S

... Whimsical Sweatshirts ...

PATRICK LOSE'S
... Whimsical Sweatshirts ...

PATRICK LOSE'S

... Whimsical Sweatshirts ...

Sterling Publishing Co., Inc. New York
A Sterling / Chapelle Book

Assistant to Patrick Lose: Lenny Houts

CHAPELLE:

Jo Packham, Owner

Cathy Sexton, Editor

Kevin Dilley, Photographer for Hazen Photography

Roxanne LeMoine, Computer Drawings for CAD ART

Staff: Malissa Boatwright, Rebecca Christensen, Cherie Hanson, Holly Hollingsworth, Susan Jorgensen, Susan Laws, Amanda McPeck, Barbara Milburn, Leslie Ridenour, Cindy Rooks, Cindy Stoeckl, and Nancy Whitley

Patrick wishes to thank the following people whose assistance and friendship made this book possible: Lenny Houts, Jean Ballard, Nora Witt, Amy Martin, and Lynn Carlisle.

All original illustrations in this book are by Patrick Lose. If you would like more information about Patrick's designs and "Out on a Whim" patterns for wearable art, quilts, wood and holiday crafts, write to: Chapelle, P.O. Box 9252, Ogden, Utah 84409.

Library of Congress Cataloging-in-Publication Data

Lose, Patrick.
    [Whimsical sweatshirts]
    Patrick Lose's whimsical sweatshirts.
          p.   cm.
    "A Sterling / Chapelle book."
    Includes index.
    ISBN 0-8069-3179-5
    1. Appliqué—Patterns. 2. Textile painting. 3. Sweatshirts.
I. Title.
TT779.L68 1995
746.9'2—dc20
                                   95-16328
                                   CIP

A Sterling/Chapelle Book

10 9 8 7 6 5 4 3 2 1

First paperback edition published in 1996 by
Sterling Publishing Company, Inc.
387 Park Avenue South, New York, N.Y. 10016
Produced by Chapelle Ltd.
P.O. Box 9252, Newgate Station, Ogden, Utah 84409
© 1995 by Chapelle Ltd.
Distributed in Canada by Sterling Publishing
c/o Canadian Manda Group, One Atlantic Avenue, Suite 105
Toronto, Ontario, Canada M6K 3E7
Distributed in Great Britain and Europe by Cassell PLC
Wellington House, 125 Strand, London WC2R 0BB, England
Distributed in Australia by Capricorn Link (Australia) Pty Ltd.
P.O. Box 6651, Baulkham Hills, Business Centre, NSW 2153, Australia
Printed and bound in Hong Kong
All rights reserved

Sterling ISBN 0-8069-3179-5 Trade
              0-8069-3180-9 Paper

For Katie . . .
I love you.

— Dad

About the author ...

PATRICK LOSE has spent his professional years in a variety of creative fields. He began his career as a costume designer for stage and screen. Costume credits include more than 50 productions and work with celebrities such as Liza Minnelli and Jane Seymour.

Today, Patrick's company, **OUT ON A WHIM**, appropriately describes his original creations. An artist and illustrator since childhood, Patrick works in many mediums. When he sits down to "doodle" at the drawing board, he never knows what one of his designs might become. Whether it's a cross-stitch piece, wearable art, a greeting card, an ornament, or a piece of furniture, he enjoys creating it all.

His crafts, clothing, and home decorating accessories have appeared frequently in national magazines, including *Better Homes and Gardens, Country Crafts, Christmas Ideas, Halloween Tricks and Treats, Folk Art Christmas, Santa Claus, Decorative Woodcrafts, Craft and Wear,* and *American Patchwork and Quilting.* Publications featuring his designs have reached over 18 million subscribers.

Contents ...

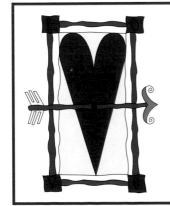

Contents ...

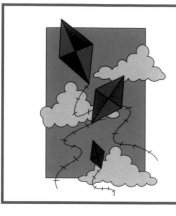

Contents ...

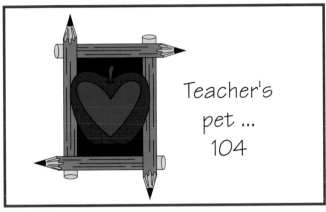

It's time to celebrate ...

Materials

Sweatshirt
Fusing adhesive, ³/₈ yard
Fabric writer, black
Fabric writer, gold
Rhinestones, asst. sizes/colors
Pencil or non-permanent pen
Scissors
Tape measure
Straight pin
Iron
Straight pin or toothpick

Fabrics for pattern pieces

By Name	By Number/Letter	Size
Clock	1	6" x 6"
Clock Face & Reflections	1A, 2A, 2D	6" x 6"
Glass Stem & Top & Mouthpiece	2B, 2C, 3A	6" x 6"
Champagne	2	2" x 4"
Horn	3	2" x 7"
Hat	4	3" x 7"
Dots on Hat & Pom-Pom	4A thru 4G, 4H	4" x 5"
Streamers (3 different colors)	5, 5A, 6, 6A, 7, 7A	2" x 6"

Instructions

1. Pre-wash the sweatshirt and all the appliqué fabrics to remove sizing and reduce shrinkage. Do not use fabric softener.

2. All the patterns in this book are the reverse of how they will appear on the sweatshirt. Lay the fusing adhesive, paper side up, onto the patterns on pages 13-15 and trace. The broken lines are positioning and/or painting lines.

3. Cut the shapes that you have traced onto the fusing adhesive apart and fuse, according to manufacturer's instructions, to the wrong sides of the appliqué fabrics. Let all fabrics cool. Do not remove paper backing yet.

4. Cut all fabric shapes out along traced pencil lines. Remove paper backing.

5. Using a pencil or non-permanent pen, transfer pattern markings and details for painting. For example: hands and dots on the clock.

6. Find the center of the sweatshirt by folding it in half down the center front. Press a slight crease to mark the center.

7. Measure 3" down from the neckline on the centerline of the sweatshirt. Mark that measurement with a straight pin. This will be the position of the piece that is closest to the neckline.

8. Referring to the photograph, position the pieces on the sweatshirt, in the following order: Clock (1), Clock Face (1A), Champagne (2), Glass Stem (2B), Reflection (2A), Streamer (5, 5A), Streamer (6, 6A), Streamer (7, 7A), Hat (4), Dots on Hat (4A, 4B, 4C, 4D, 4E, 4F, 4G), Pom-Pom (4H), Horn (3), Mouthpiece (3A), Glass Top (2C), and Reflection (2D). Fuse all pieces at once according to manufacturer's instructions.

9. Using a gold fabric writer, outline the raw edges of all the appliqué pieces, beginning at the upper left-hand side if you are right-handed or at the upper right-hand side if you are left-handed. As you go, scatter the rhinestones and set each one in place by using a thick dot of paint and sinking each rhinestone into the center of each paint dot. Push the rhinestone down gently. Continue down the front of the sweatshirt with the gold fabric writer until you get to the clock face. Using a black fabric writer, paint the clock face. Using the gold fabric writer, finish painting the design and placing the rhinestones as you go. You may also choose to embellish with additional painted lines. Use a steady hand and constant pressure on the bottle—any stray paint splatters can easily be removed with a straight pin or toothpick.

10. Dry flat for 4 to 6 hours. The paint will cure completely in 24 hours and the sweatshirt can be washed after 72 hours. To launder, turn the sweatshirt inside out and wash in warm water on delicate cycle. Tumble-dry on low heat.

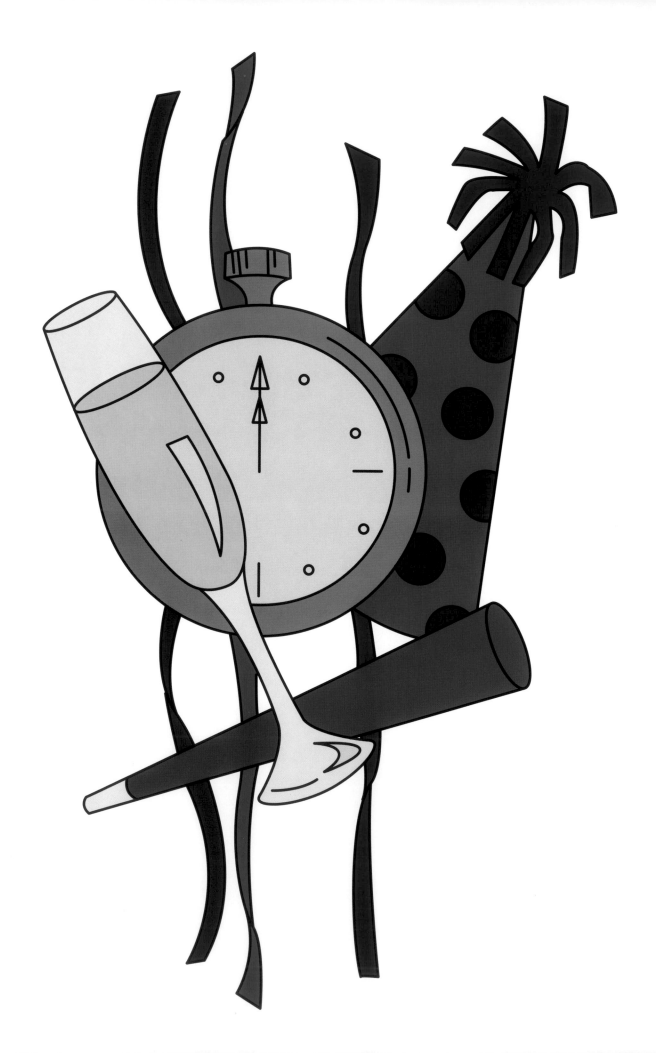

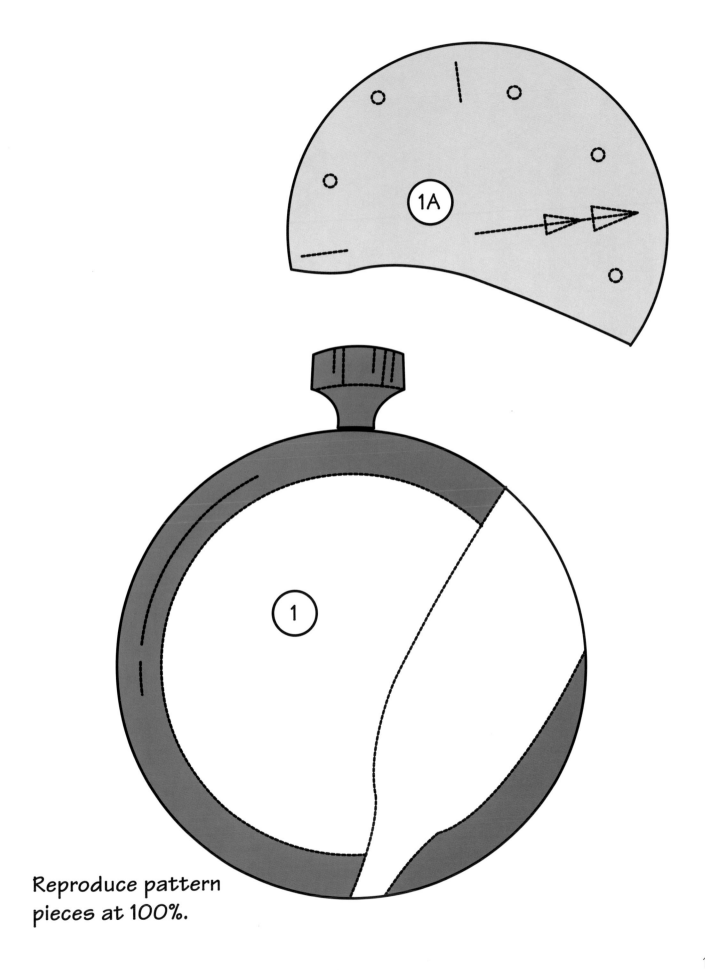

Reproduce pattern
pieces at 100%.

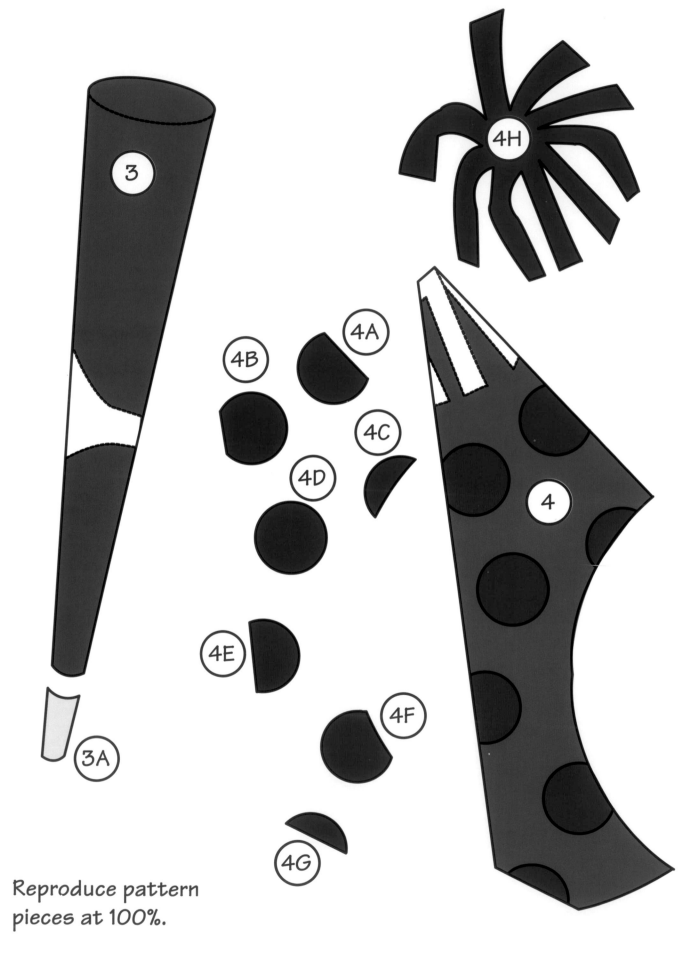

Reproduce pattern
pieces at 100%.

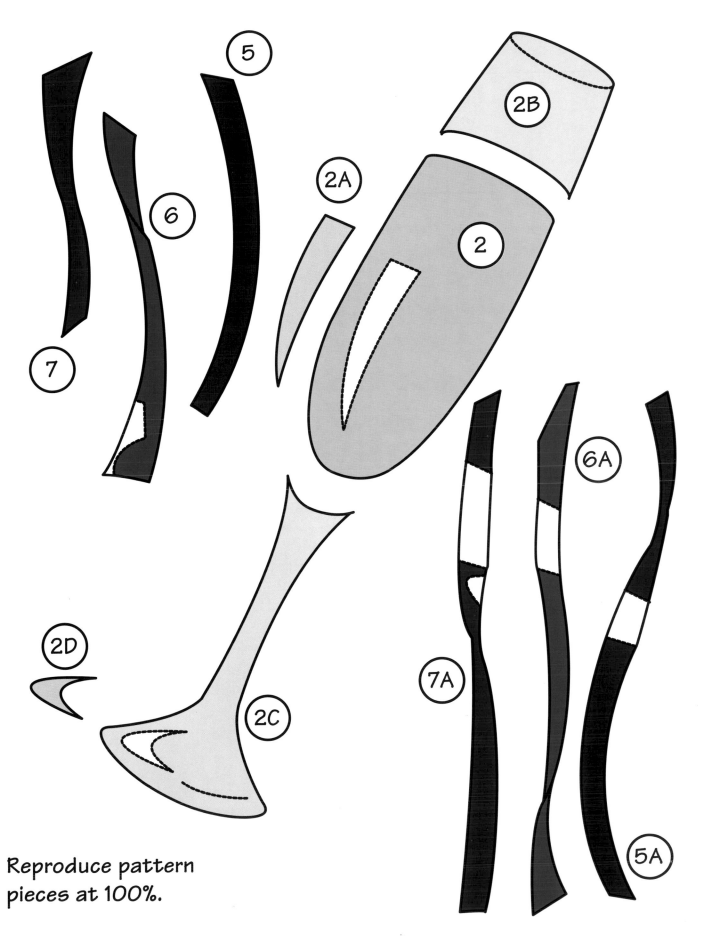

Reproduce pattern
pieces at 100%.

Let it snow ...

Materials

Sweatshirt
Fusing adhesive, 3/8 yard
Fabric writer, black
Fabric writer, gold
Pencil or non-permanent pen
Scissors
Tape measure
Straight pin
Iron
Straight pin or toothpick

Fabrics for pattern pieces

By Name	By Number/Letter	Size
Snowman	1	7" x 10"
Carrot	1A	2" x 2"
Tie	1B	2" x 2"
Vest	1C	4" x 5"
Pockets, Hat, Broom Binding	1D, 2A, 4C	3" x 4"
Hat Band	2B	2" x 2"
Snowflakes	3A thru 3C	8" x 8"
Broomstick	4B	2" x 4"
Broom	4A	3" x 5"

Instructions

1. Pre-wash the sweatshirt and all the appliqué fabrics to remove sizing and reduce shrinkage. Do not use fabric softener.

2. All the patterns in this book are the reverse of how they will appear on the sweatshirt. Lay the fusing adhesive, paper side up, onto the patterns on pages 19-21 and trace. The broken lines are positioning and/or painting lines.

3. Cut the shapes that you have traced onto the fusing adhesive apart and fuse, according to manufacturer's instructions, to the wrong sides of the appliqué fabrics. Let all fabrics cool. Do not remove paper backing yet.

4. Cut all fabric shapes out along traced pencil lines. Remove paper backing.

5. Using a pencil or non-permanent pen, transfer pattern markings and details for painting. For example: mouth, eyes and hand details, and vest buttons.

6. Find the center of the sweatshirt by folding it in half down the center front. Press a slight crease to mark the center.

7. Measure 3" down from the neckline on the centerline of the sweatshirt. Mark that measurement with a straight pin. This will be the position of the piece that is closest to the neckline.

8. Referring to the photograph, position the pieces on the sweatshirt, in the following order: Snowman (1), Carrot (1A), Tie (1B), Vest (1C), Pockets (1D), Hat (2A), Hat Band (2B), Snowflakes (3A, 3B, 3C), Broomstick (4B), Broom (4A), and Broom Binding (4C). Fuse all pieces at once according to manufacturer's instructions.

9. Using a gold fabric writer, outline the raw edges of all the appliqué pieces, beginning at the upper left-hand side if you are right-handed or at the upper right-hand side if you are left-handed. Continue down the front of the sweatshirt with the gold fabric writer until you get to the snowman's face. Using a black fabric writer, paint the eyes and the mouth. Using the gold fabric writer, finish painting the design. You may also choose to embellish with additional painted lines. Use a steady hand and constant pressure on the bottle —any stray paint splatters can easily be removed with a straight pin or toothpick.

10. Dry flat for 4 to 6 hours. The paint will cure completely in 24 hours and the sweatshirt can be washed after 72 hours. To launder, turn the sweatshirt inside out and wash in warm water on delicate cycle. Tumble-dry on low heat.

1

Reproduce pattern
pieces at 100%.

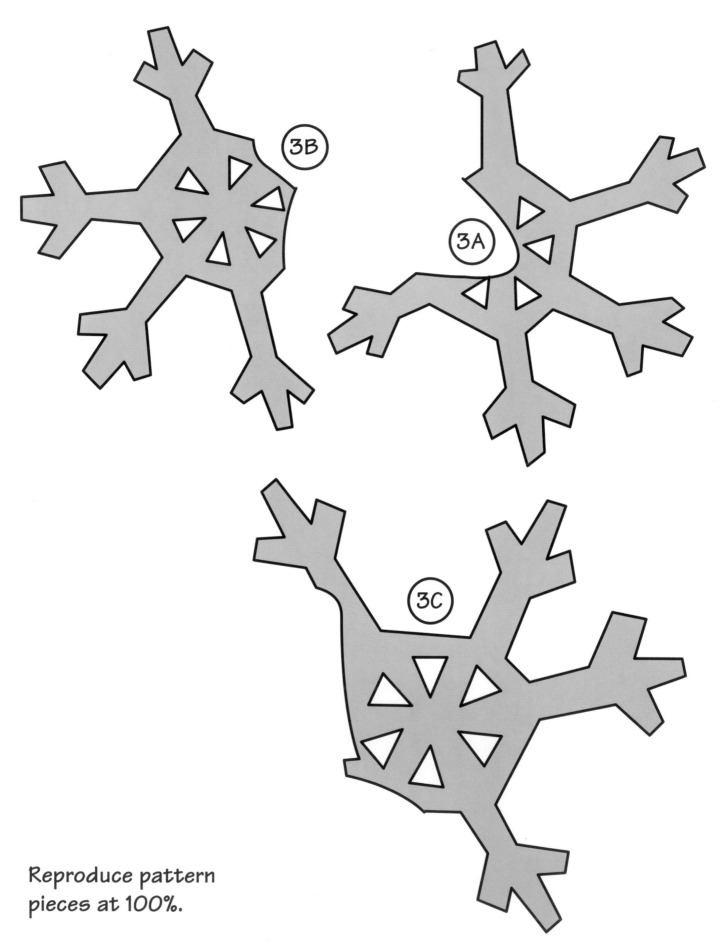

Reproduce pattern
pieces at 100%.

4A

2B

1B

4C

4B

1A

1D

Reproduce pattern
pieces at 100%.

Love struck ...

<table>
<tr><td colspan="2">

Materials

100% cotton sheeting shirt
Fusing adhesive, 3/8 yard
Fabric writer, gold
Pencil or non-permanent pen
Scissors
Tape measure
Iron
Straight pin or toothpick

</td></tr>
</table>

Fabrics for pattern pieces

By Name	By Number/Letter	Size
Background	1	6" x 11"
Corner Boxes	2 thru 5	3" x 3"
Frame	6 thru 9	3" x 12"
Heart	10	5" x 11"
Arrow	11 and 12	2" x 5"
Arrowhead	13	2" x 3"
Arrow Tail	14	2" x 3"

Instructions

1. Pre-wash the shirt and all the appliqué fabrics to remove sizing and reduce shrinkage. Do not use fabric softener.

2. All the patterns in this book are the reverse of how they will appear on the shirt. Lay the fusing adhesive, paper side up, onto the patterns on pages 25-27 and trace. The broken lines are positioning and/or painting lines.

3. Cut the shapes that you have traced onto the fusing adhesive apart and fuse, according to manufacturer's instructions, to the wrong sides of the appliqué fabrics. Let all fabrics cool. Do not remove paper backing yet.

4. Cut all fabric shapes out along traced pencil lines. Remove paper backing.

5. Using a pencil or non-permanent pen, transfer pattern markings and details for painting. For example: arrow details and letters in the corner boxes.

6. Find the center of the shirt by folding it in half down the center front. Press a slight crease to mark the center.

7. Position the background (1) on the shirt front. Fold this piece in half, matching the long sides, and make a crease in the top and bottom with your fingers. Match this crease with the crease on the front of the shirt to center the design. Piece 1

should be placed about 3" down from the neckline. Fuse piece 1 in place according to manufacturer's instructions.

8. Referring to the photograph, position the remaining pieces on the shirt, in the following order: Heart (10), Corner Boxes (2, 3, 4, 5), Frame (6, 7, 8, 9), Arrow (11, 12), Arrowhead (13), and Arrow Tail (14). For the frame pieces (6, 7, 8, 9), use the pattern on page 27 and cut out four. Position these pieces on the shirt and trim to the appropriate lengths for the top, bottom, right side, and left side of the frame. Fuse all pieces at once according to manufacturer's instructions.

9. Using a gold fabric writer, outline the raw edges of all the appliqué pieces, beginning at the upper left-hand side if you are right-handed or at the upper right-hand side if you are left-handed. You may also choose to embellish with additional painted lines. Use a steady hand and constant pressure on the bottle—any stray paint splatters can easily be removed with a straight pin or toothpick.

10. Dry flat for 4 to 6 hours. The paint will cure completely in 24 hours and the shirt can be washed after 72 hours. To launder, turn the shirt inside out and wash in warm water on delicate cycle. Tumble dry on low heat.

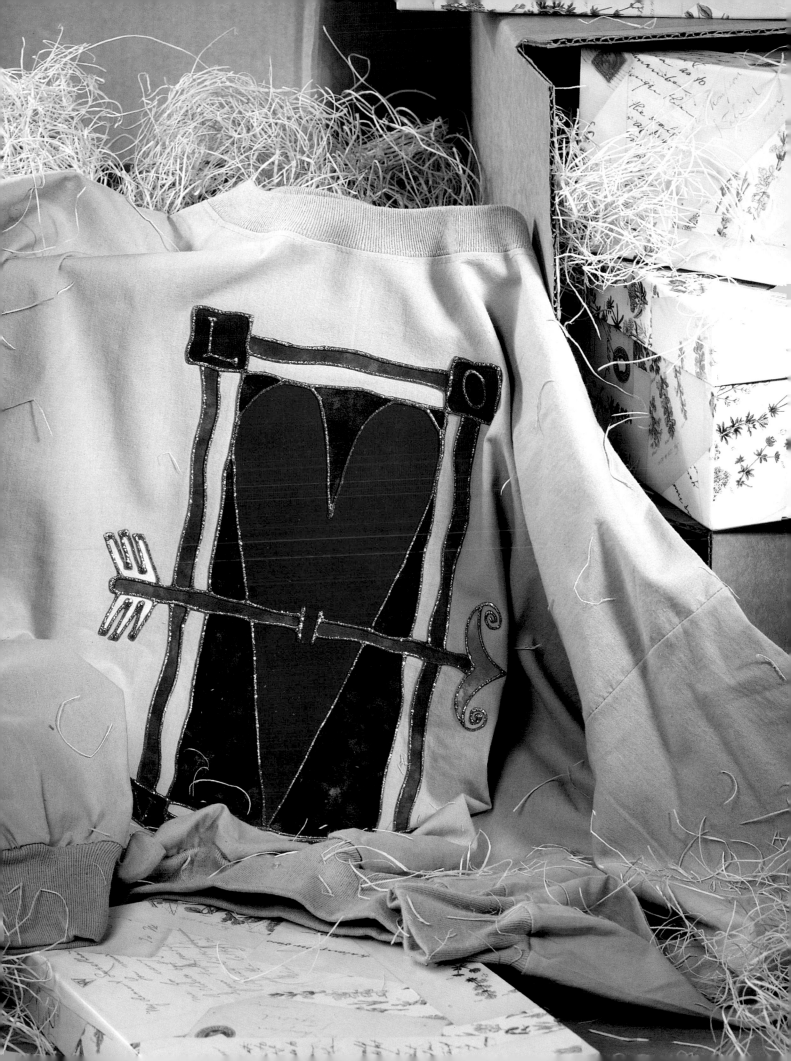

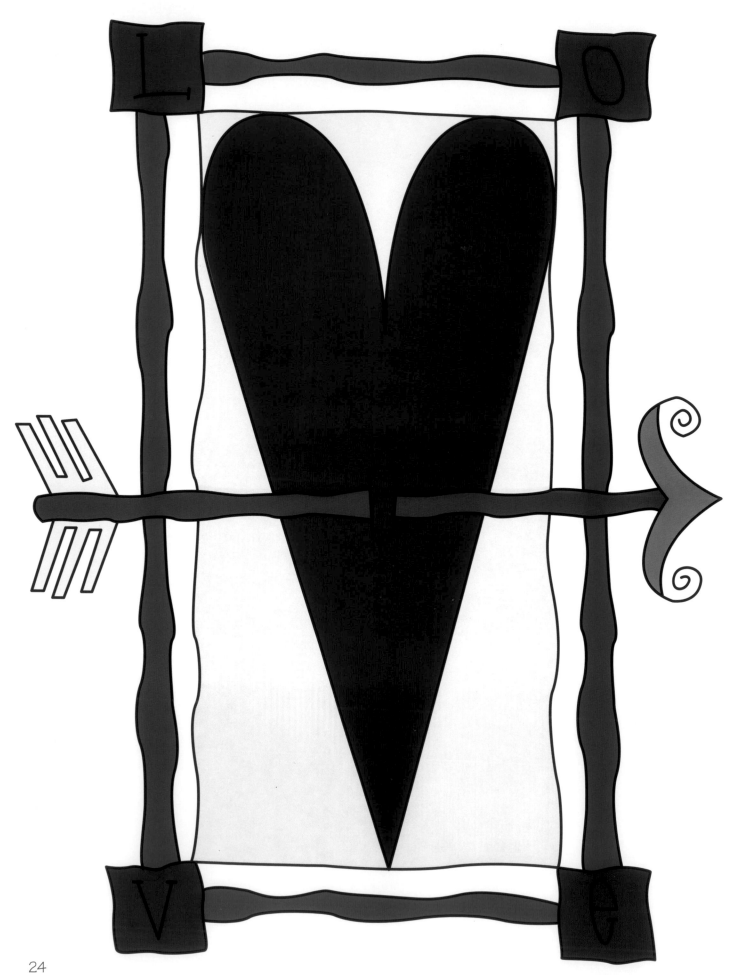

24

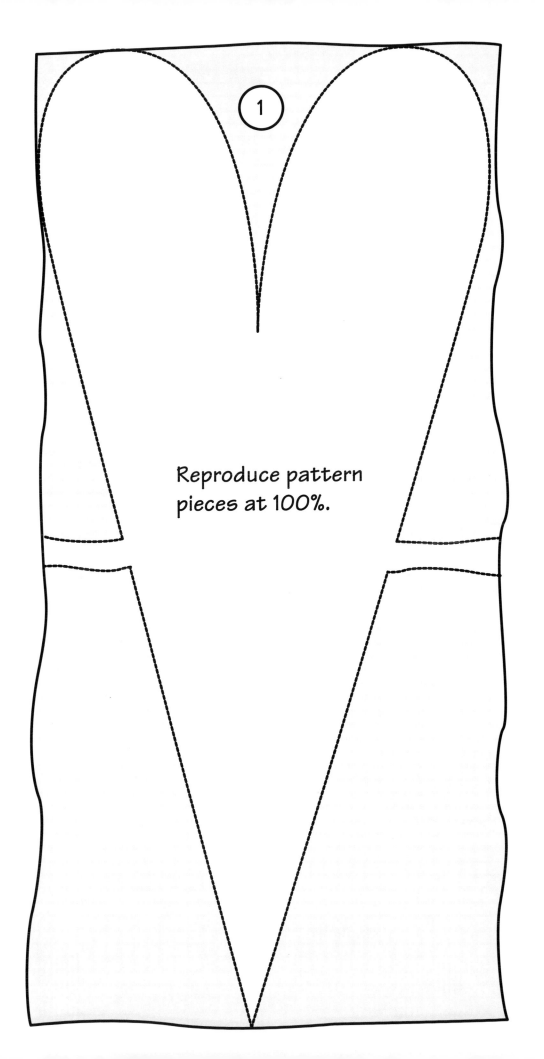

Reproduce pattern
pieces at 100%.

Reproduce pattern
pieces at 100%.

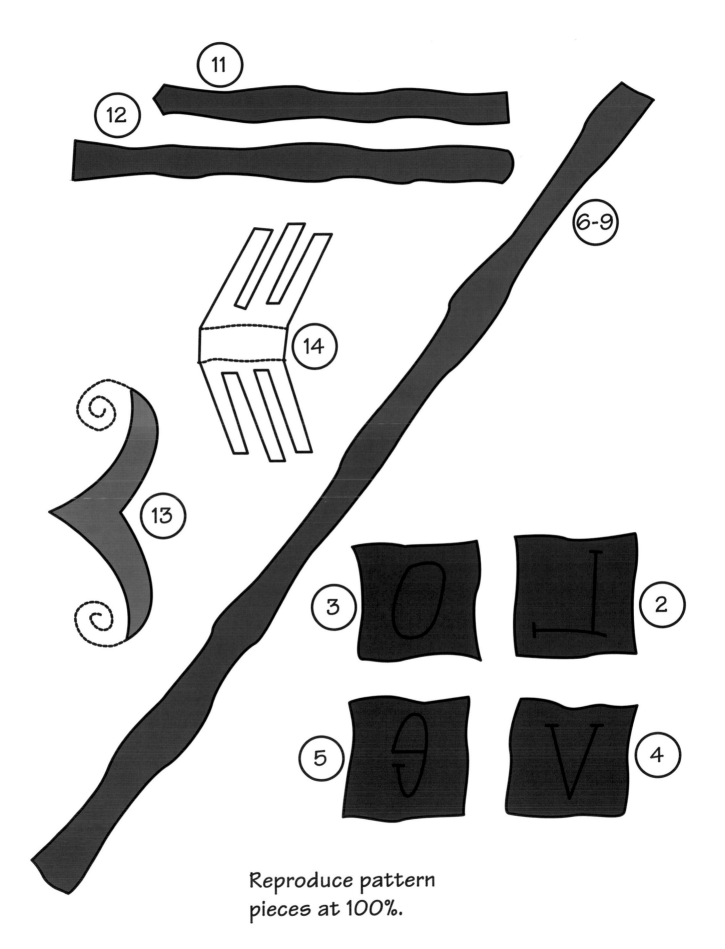

Reproduce pattern
pieces at 100%.

Friendship ...

Materials

- Sweatshirt
- Fusing adhesive, ½ yard
- Fabric writer, gold
- Rhinestones, asst. sizes/colors
- Pencil or non-permanent pen
- Scissors
- Tape measure
- Iron
- Straight pin or toothpick

Fabrics for pattern pieces

By Name	By Number/Letter	Size
Background	1	10" x 14"
Hearts	2	9" x 12"
Stars	3A thru 3C	7" x 10"

Instructions

1. Pre-wash the sweatshirt and all the appliqué fabrics to remove sizing and reduce shrinkage. Do not use fabric softener.

2. All the patterns in this book are the reverse of how they will appear on the sweatshirt. Lay the fusing adhesive, paper side up, onto the patterns from pages 31-33 (after they have been enlarged 133%) and trace. The broken lines are positioning and/or painting lines.

3. Cut the shapes that you have traced onto the fusing adhesive apart and fuse, according to manufacturer's instructions, to the wrong sides of the appliqué fabrics. Let all fabrics cool. Do not remove paper backing yet.

4. Cut all fabric shapes out along traced pencil lines. Remove paper backing.

5. Find the center of the sweatshirt by folding it in half down the center front. Press a slight crease to mark the center.

6. Position the background (1) on the sweatshirt front. Fold this piece in half, matching the long sides, and make a crease in the top and bottom with your fingers. Match this crease with the crease on the front of the sweatshirt to center the design. Piece 1 should be placed about 3" down from the neckline. Fuse piece 1 in place according to manufacturer's instructions.

7. Referring to the photograph, position the remaining pieces on the sweatshirt, in the following order: Hearts (2) and Stars (3A, 3B, 3C). Fuse all pieces at once according to manufacturer's instructions.

8. Using a gold fabric writer, outline the raw edges of all the appliqué pieces, beginning at the upper left-hand side if you are right-handed or at the upper right-hand side if you are left-handed. As you go, scatter the rhinestones and set each one in place by using a thick dot of paint and sinking each rhinestone into the center of each paint dot. Push the rhinestone down gently. Use a steady hand and constant pressure on the bottle—any stray paint splatters can easily be removed with a straight pin or toothpick.

9. Dry flat for 4 to 6 hours. The paint will cure completely in 24 hours and the sweatshirt can be washed after 72 hours. To launder, turn the sweatshirt inside out and wash in warm water on delicate cycle. Tumble-dry on low heat.

Reproduce
pattern
pieces at
133%.

1

2

Reproduce pattern
pieces at 133%.

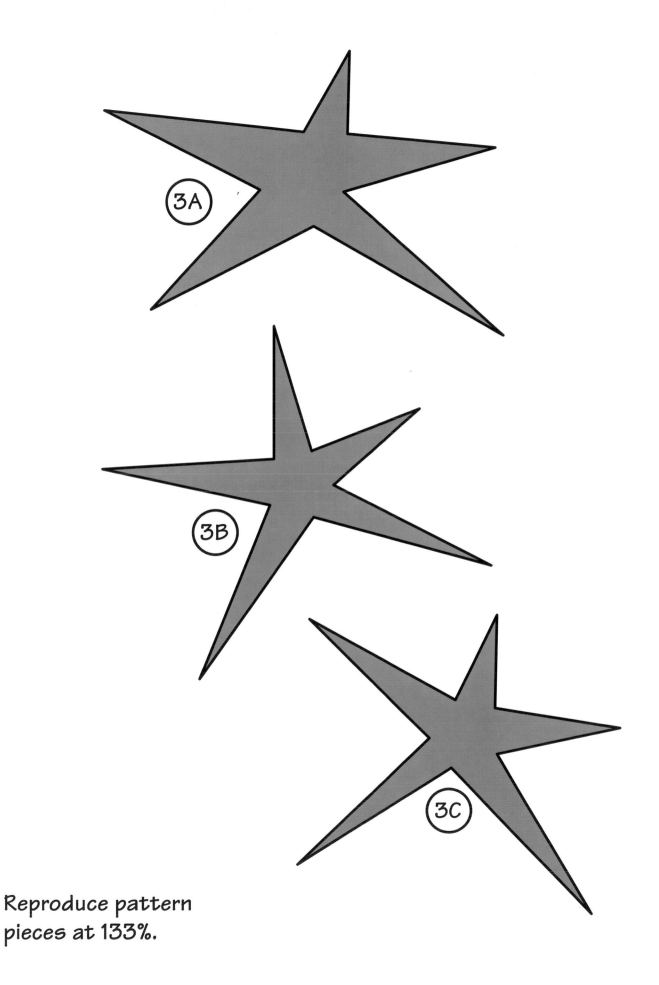

Reproduce pattern
pieces at 133%.

Luck of the Irish ...

Materials

- Sweatshirt
- Fusing adhesive, 3/8 yard
- Fabric writer, gold
- Pencil or non-permanent pen
- Scissors
- Tape measure
- Straight pins
- Sewing machine
- Thread for binding
- Iron
- Straight pin or toothpick

Fabrics for pattern pieces

By Name	By Number/Letter	Size
Shamrocks & Binding	1	1/2 yard
Hearts	2	10" x 10"

Instructions

1. Pre-wash the sweatshirt and all the appliqué fabrics to remove sizing and reduce shrinkage. Do not use fabric softener.

2. All the patterns in this book are the reverse of how they will appear on the sweatshirt. Lay the fusing adhesive, paper side up, onto the patterns on page 36 and trace.

3. Cut the shapes that you have traced onto the fusing adhesive apart and fuse, according to manufacturer's instructions, to the wrong sides of the appliqué fabrics. Let all fabrics cool. Do not remove paper backing yet.

4. Cut all fabric shapes out along traced pencil lines. Remove paper backing.

5. Cut the ribbing around the waist of the sweatshirt off. Lay the sweatshirt flat and make sure that the bottom is cut straight.

6. For the binding around the bottom of the sweatshirt, cut enough bias strips 2" wide to equal approximately 47" for a medium-sized sweatshirt (a little less for smaller sizes and a little more for larger sizes). Piece these bias strips together by placing the ends, right sides together, at right angles and stitching the ends with a diagonal or mitered seam. See Diagram A on page 142.

7. To bind the sweatshirt, press one long side of the binding 3/8". Beginning at one of the side seams on the lower edge of the sweatshirt, place the binding strip on the sweatshirt, right sides together, aligning the raw edge of the sweatshirt to the long raw edge of the binding. Fold over 1/2" at the beginning of the binding. Stitch the binding around the shirt, through all layers, using a 3/8" seam allowance.

8. When you get all the way around the sweatshirt, overlap the binding strips beyond the fold where you started. Trim off excess binding.

9. Turn the other folded edge of the binding strip over the raw edge of the sweatshirt to the inside. Fold the folded edge to the underside of the binding and pin securely around sweatshirt on the inside. Top-stitch in the "ditch" or seam of the binding on the outside of the shirt with matching thread and a matching bobbin thread.

10. Measure up from the binding 1 1/2" and position a shamrock. Continue around the bottom of the sweatshirt, alternating shamrocks (1) and hearts (2). Fuse all pieces according to manufacturer's instructions. If you have chosen not to bind the sweatshirt, simply raise the shamrocks (1) and hearts (2) up on the sweatshirt approximately 8".

11. Using a gold fabric writer, outline the raw edges of all the appliqué pieces. Because the shamrocks and hearts are placed all the way around the bottom of the sweatshirt, you have to paint them in stages. Allow the paint to dry for 4 to 6 hours before continuing. Use a steady hand and constant pressure on the bottle—any stray paint splatters can easily be removed with a straight pin or toothpick.

12. Dry flat for 4 to 6 hours. The paint will cure completely in 24 hours and the sweatshirt can be washed after 72 hours. To launder, turn the sweatshirt inside out and wash in warm water on delicate cycle. Tumble-dry on low heat.

Reproduce pattern
pieces at 100%.

36

Reproduce pattern
pieces at 100%.

Bunnies & carrots ...

Materials

- Sweatshirt
- Fusing adhesive, 1/4 yard
- Fabric writer, black
- Fabric writer, orange
- Fabric writer, green
- Pencil or non-permanent pen
- Scissors
- Tape measure
- Iron
- Straight pin or toothpick

Fabrics for pattern pieces

By Name	By Number/Letter	Size
Bunnies (cut 3, reverse 1)	1	7" x 11"
Carrots (cut 3, reverse 1)	2A	4" x 5"
Carrot Tops (cut 3, reverse 1)	2B	3" x 3"

Instructions

1. Pre-wash the sweatshirt and all the appliqué fabrics to remove sizing and reduce shrinkage. Do not use fabric softener.

2. All the patterns in this book are the reverse of how they will appear on the sweatshirt. Lay the fusing adhesive, paper side up, onto the patterns on page 37 and trace. The broken lines are positioning and/or painting lines.

3. Cut the shapes that you have traced onto the fusing adhesive apart and fuse, according to manufacturer's instructions, to the wrong sides of the appliqué fabrics. Let all fabrics cool. Do not remove paper backing yet.

4. Cut all fabric shapes out along traced pencil lines. Remove paper backing.

5. Using a pencil or non-permanent pen, transfer pattern markings and details for painting. For example: carrot and bunny details.

6. If you choose to position your pattern pieces as we've done, position the three bunnies (1) on the front of the sweatshirt. Do not fuse yet. If you choose to create your own design with the pattern pieces, go to Step 8.

7. Referring to the photograph, position the remaining pieces on the sweatshirt, in the following order: Carrots (2A) and Carrot Tops (2B). Slip the carrots under the bunnies, then add the carrot tops to the top of the carrots. If your bunny fabric is lighter in color than your carrot fabric, draw a line with a pencil where the bunny meets the carrot and cut the section that falls underneath the bunny away. Slip the carrot pieces under the bunny 1/8". Fuse all pieces at once according to manu-facturer's instructions.

8. Using a green fabric writer, outline the raw edges of all the carrot top appliqué pieces. Using an orange fabric writer, outline the raw edges of the top parts of the carrots. Using a black fabric writer, outline the raw edges of the bunnies and dot the eyes. Using the orange fabric writer, continue by outlining the raw edges of the bottom parts of the carrots. You may also choose to embellish with additional painted lines. Use a steady hand and constant pressure on the bottle—any stray paint splatters can easily be removed with a straight pin or toothpick.

9. Dry flat for 4 to 6 hours. The paint will cure completely in 24 hours and the sweatshirt can be washed after 72 hours. To launder, turn the sweatshirt inside out and wash in warm water on delicate cycle. Tumble-dry on low heat.

Easter's on its way ...

Materials

100% cotton sheeting shirt
Fusing adhesive, $3/8$ yard
Fabric writer, black
Fabric writer, gold
Pencil or non-permanent pen
Scissors
Tape measure
Iron
Straight pin or toothpick

Fabrics for pattern pieces

By Name	By Number/Letter	Size
Background	1	6" x 8"
Frame (cut 2 each)	2A	8" x 8"
Squiggles (cut 2 each)	2B	4" x 8"
Bunny	3	5" x 9"
Corner Boxes (cut 4)	4	6" x 6"
Egg & Egg Stripes	5A and 5B	2" x 4"
Egg & Egg Stripes	5A and 5B	2" x 4"
Egg & Egg Dots	5A and 5C	2" x 4"
Egg & Egg Dots	5A and 5C	2" x 4"

Instructions

1. Pre-wash the shirt and all the appliqué fabrics to remove sizing and reduce shrinkage. Do not use fabric softener.

2. All the patterns in this book are the reverse of how they will appear on the shirt. Lay the fusing adhesive, paper side up, onto the patterns on pages 43-45 and trace. The broken lines are positioning and/or painting lines.

3. Cut the shapes that you have traced onto the fusing adhesive apart and fuse, according to manufacturer's instructions, to the wrong sides of the appliqué fabrics. Let all fabrics cool. Do not remove paper backing yet.

4. Cut all fabric shapes out along traced pencil lines. Remove paper backing.

5. Using a pencil or non-permanent pen, transfer pattern markings and details for painting. For example: bunny's detail, eye, and nose.

6. Find the center of the shirt by folding it in half down the center front. Press a slight crease to mark the center.

7. Position the background (1) on the shirt front. Fold this piece in half, matching the long sides, and make a crease in the top and bottom with your fingers. Match this crease with the crease on the front of the shirt to center the design. Piece 1 should be placed about 5" down from the neckline. Fuse piece 1 in place according to manufacturer's instructions.

8. Referring to the photograph, position the remaining pieces on the shirt, in the following order: Frame (2A), Squiggles (2B), Bunny (3), Corner Boxes (4), Eggs, Egg Stripes, and Egg Dots (5A, 5B, 5C). Fuse all pieces at once according to manufacturer's instructions.

9. Using a gold fabric writer, outline the raw edges of all the appliqué pieces, beginning at the upper left-hand side if you are right-handed or at the upper right-hand side if you are left-handed. Using a black fabric writer, dot the bunny's eye. You may also choose to embellish with additional painted lines. Use a steady hand and constant pressure on the bottle—any stray paint splatters can easily be removed with a straight pin or toothpick.

10. Dry flat for 4 to 6 hours. The paint will cure completely in 24 hours and the shirt can be washed after 72 hours. To launder, turn the shirt inside out and wash in warm water on delicate cycle. Tumble dry on low heat.

Reproduce pattern
pieces at 100%.

3

5A

5C

Reproduce pattern
pieces at 100%.

Reproduce pattern
pieces at 100%.

Birds of a feather ...

Materials

100% cotton sheeting shirt
Fusing adhesive, ³/₈ yard
Fabric writer, black
Fabric writer, gold
Pencil or non-permanent pen
Scissors
Tape measure
Iron
Straight pin or toothpick

Fabrics for pattern pieces

By Name	By Number/Letter	Size
Background	1	9" x 12"
Birdhouse	2	6" x 9"
Holes (cut 2) & Roof	2A, 2C	5" x 9"
Birdhouse Base & Roof Peak	2B, 2D	4" x 7"
Pole	3	2" x 3"
Birds (cut 2, reverse 1)	4	4" x 8"
Beaks (cut 2, reverse 1)	4A	2" x 2"

Instructions

1. Pre-wash the shirt and all the appliqué fabrics to remove sizing and reduce shrinkage. Do not use fabric softener.

2. All the patterns in this book are the reverse of how they will appear on the shirt. Lay the fusing adhesive, paper side up, onto the patterns from pages 49-51 (after they have been enlarged 117%) and trace. The broken lines are positioning and/or painting lines.

3. Cut the shapes that you have traced onto the fusing adhesive apart and fuse, according to manufacturer's instructions, to the wrong sides of the appliqué fabrics. Let all fabrics cool. Do not remove paper backing yet.

4. Cut all fabric shapes out along traced pencil lines. Remove paper backing.

5. Using a pencil or non-permanent pen, transfer pattern markings and details for painting. For example: bird legs and wing details.

6. Find the center of the shirt by folding it in half down the center front. Press a slight crease to mark the center.

7. Position the background (1) on the shirt front. Fold this piece in half, matching the long sides, and make a crease in the top and bottom with your fingers. Match this crease with the crease on the front of the shirt to center the design. Piece 1 should be placed about 3" down from the neckline. Fuse piece 1 in place according to manufacturer's instructions.

8. Referring to the photograph, position the remaining pieces on the shirt, in the following order: Birdhouse (2), Roof (2C), Birdhouse Base (2B), Pole (3), Holes (2A), Roof Peak (2D), first Bird (4), Bird Beak (4A), second Bird (4), and Bird Beak (4A). Fuse all pieces at once according to manufacturer's instructions.

9. Using a gold fabric writer, paint small dots around the outside edge of the background (1), beginning at the upper left-hand side if you are right-handed or at the upper right-hand side if you are left-handed. Make sure you leave a small space—about ¹/₈"—between each dot. If you get them too close together, they will "bleed" into each other. Continue down the front of the shirt with the gold fabric writer until you get to the first bird's legs. Using a black fabric writer, paint this bird's legs. Continue down the front of the shirt with the gold fabric writer until you get to the second bird's legs. Using the black fabric writer, paint this bird's legs. Using the gold fabric writer, finish painting the design. You may also choose to embellish with additional painted lines. Use a steady hand and constant pressure on the bottle—any stray paint splatters can easily be removed with a straight pin or toothpick.

10. Dry flat for 4 to 6 hours. The paint will cure completely in 24 hours and the shirt can be washed after 72 hours. To launder, turn the shirt inside out and wash in warm water on delicate cycle. Tumble dry on low heat.

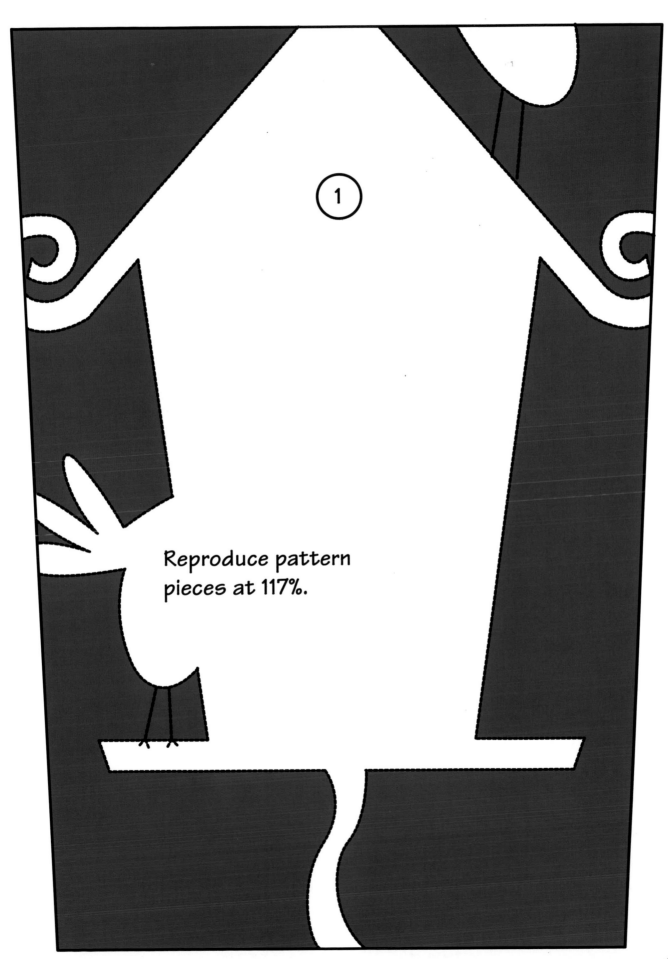

Reproduce pattern
pieces at 117%.

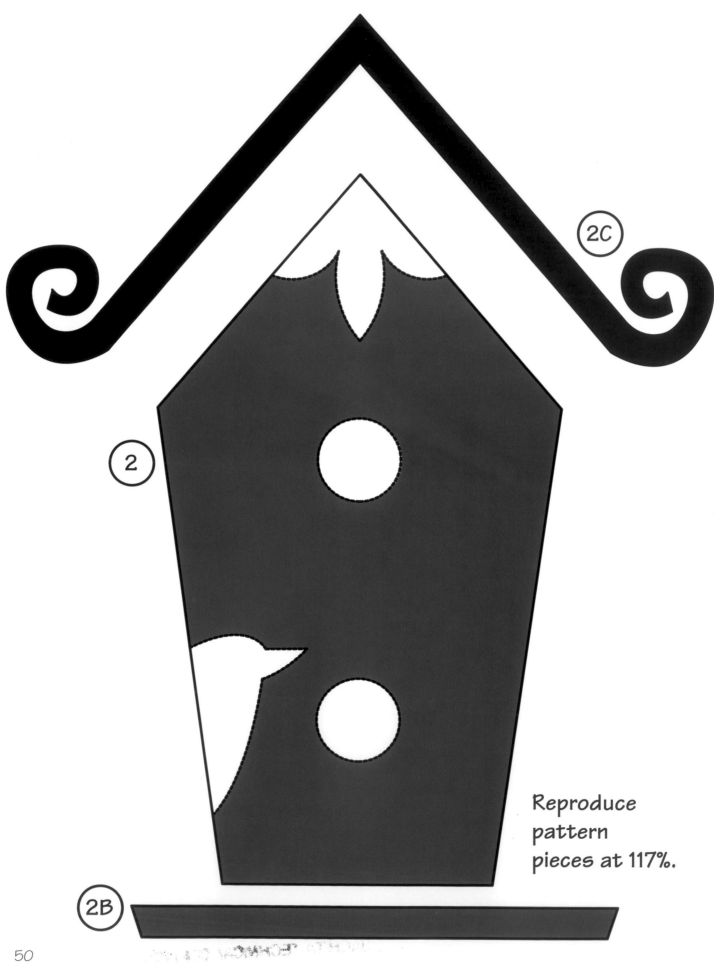

2C

2

Reproduce
pattern
pieces at 117%.

2B

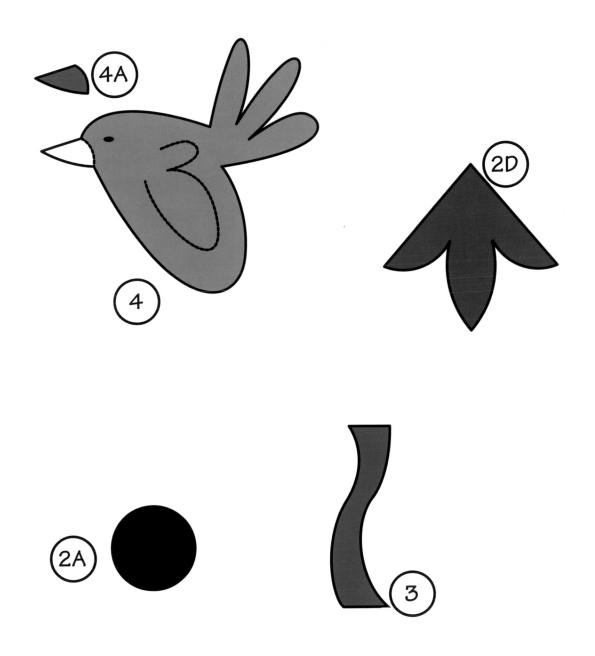

4A

2D

4

2A

3

Reproduce pattern
pieces at 117%.

Fly a kite ...

Materials

100% cotton sheeting shirt
Fusing adhesive, $^3/_8$ yard
Fabric writer, gold
Pencil or non-permanent pen
Scissors
Tape measure
Iron
Straight pin or toothpick

Fabrics for pattern pieces

By Name	By Number/Letter	Size
Background	1	8" x 12"
Clouds	2 thru 4	7" x 10"
Kite	5A and 5D	2" x 3"
Kite	5B and 5C	2" x 3"
Kite	6A and 6D	2" x 3"
Kite	6B and 6C	2" x 3"
Kite	7A and 7D	2" x 2"
Kite	7B and 7C	2" x 2"

Instructions

1. Pre-wash the shirt and all the appliqué fabrics to remove sizing and reduce shrinkage. Do not use fabric softener.

2. All the patterns in this book are the reverse of how they will appear on the shirt. Lay the fusing adhesive, paper side up, onto the patterns from pages 55-57 (after they have been enlarged 133%) and trace. The broken lines are positioning and/or painting lines.

3. Cut the shapes that you have traced onto the fusing adhesive apart and fuse, according to manufacturer's instructions, to the wrong sides of the appliqué fabrics. Let all fabrics cool. Do not remove paper backing yet.

4. Cut all fabric shapes out along traced pencil lines. Remove paper backing.

5. Using a pencil or non-permanent pen, transfer pattern markings and details for painting. For example: kite tails and ties.

6. Find the center of the shirt by folding it in half down the center front. Press a slight crease to mark the center.

7. Position the background (1) on the shirt front. Fold this piece in half, matching the long sides, and make a crease in the top and bottom with your fingers. Match this crease with the crease on the front of the shirt to center the design. Piece 1 should be placed about 3" down from the neckline. Fuse piece 1 in place according to manufacturer's instructions.

8. Referring to the photograph, position the remaining pieces on the shirt, in the following order: Clouds (2, 3, 4), Kite (5A, 5B, 5C, 5D), Kite (6A, 6B, 6C, 6D), and Kite (7A, 7B, 7C, 7D). Fuse all pieces at once according to manufacturer's instructions.

9. Using a gold fabric writer, outline the raw edges of all the appliqué pieces, beginning at the upper left-hand side if you are right-handed or at the upper right-hand side if you are left-handed. You may also choose to embellish with additional painted lines. Use a steady hand and constant pressure on the bottle—any stray paint splatters can easily be removed with a straight pin or toothpick.

10. Dry flat for 4 to 6 hours. The paint will cure completely in 24 hours and the shirt can be washed after 72 hours. To launder, turn the shirt inside out and wash in warm water on delicate cycle. Tumble dry on low heat.

Reproduce pattern
pieces at 133%.

Reproduce pattern
pieces at 133%.

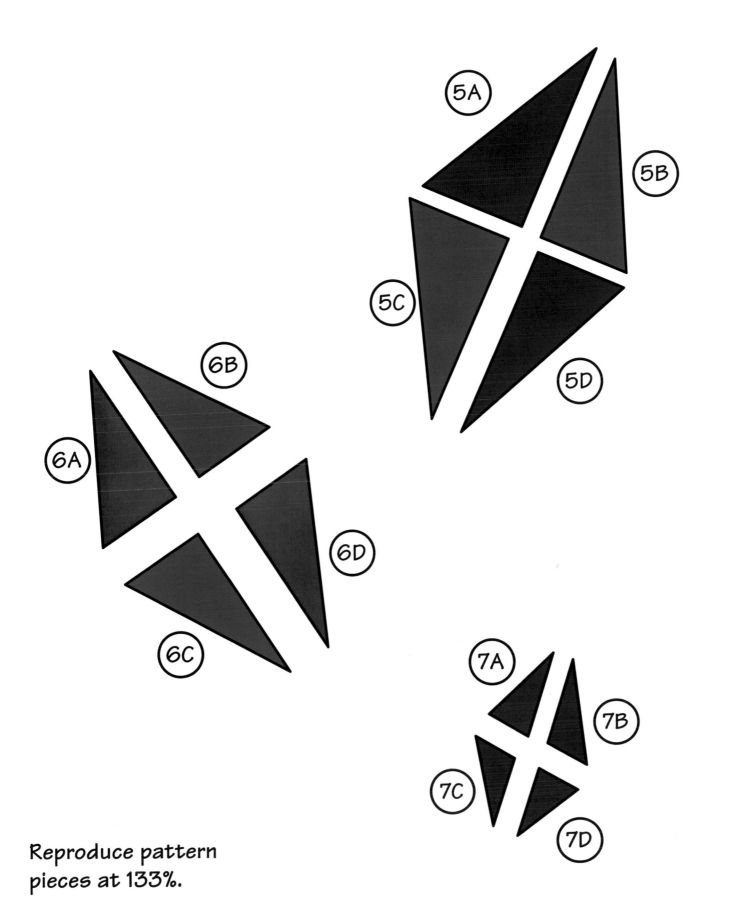

Reproduce pattern
pieces at 133%.

How does your garden grow? ...

Materials

100% cotton sheeting shirt
Fusing adhesive, ³/₈ yard
Fabric writer, gold
Pencil or non-permanent pen
Scissors
Tape measure
Iron
Tracing paper
Straight pin or toothpick
Iron-on transfer pencil

Fabrics for pattern pieces

By Name	By Number/Letter	Size
Backgrounds	1, 2, 6	6" x 11"
Background & Flower Centers	3, 1B, 2B, 6B	4" x 5"
Backgrounds & Foliage	4, 5, 1C, 6C	8" x 8"
Flower	1A	3" x 3"
Flower	2A	3" x 5"
Heart & Ladybug Wings	3A, 4A, 5A	5" x 5"
Ladybug Heads	4B, 5B	2" x 2"
Flower	6A	3" x 3"

Instructions

1. Pre-wash the shirt and all the appliqué fabrics to remove sizing and reduce shrinkage. Do not use fabric softener.

2. All the patterns in this book are the reverse of how they will appear on the shirt. Lay the fusing adhesive, paper side up, onto the patterns on pages 61-63 and trace. The broken lines are positioning and/or painting lines.

3. Cut the shapes that you have traced onto the fusing adhesive apart and fuse, according to manufacturer's instructions, to the wrong sides of the appliqué fabrics. Let all fabrics cool. Do not remove paper backing yet.

4. Cut all fabric shapes out along traced pencil lines. Remove paper backing.

5. Using a pencil or non-permanent pen, transfer pattern markings and details for painting. For example: flower petal lines and ladybug wings.

6. Find the center of the shirt by folding it in half down the center front. Press a slight crease to mark the center.

7. Position the backgrounds (1, 2, 3, 4, 5, 6) on the shirt front about 3" down from the neckline. Center the pieces on the shirt parallel with the crease on the front of the shirt. Fuse pieces in place according to manufacturer's instructions.

8. Referring to the photograph, position the remaining pieces on the shirt, in the following order: Flower (1A), Flower Center (1B), Flower (2A), Flower Center (2B), Heart (3A), Ladybug Wings (4A), Ladybug Heads (4B), Ladybug Wings (5A), Ladybug Heads (5B), Flower (6A), Flower Center (6B), and Foliage (1C, 6C). Fuse all pieces at once according to manufacturer's instructions.

9. Transfer the lettering to your shirt by laying the piece of tracing paper over the lettering pattern and trace over it with an iron-on transfer pencil. Turn the traced pattern, transfer pencil side down, on your shirt and press it on using a warm iron.

10. Using a gold fabric writer, outline the raw edges of all the appliqué pieces, beginning at the upper left-hand side if you are right-handed or at the upper right-hand side if you are left-handed. You may also choose to embellish with additional painted lines. Use a steady hand and constant pressure on the bottle—any stray paint splatters can easily be removed with a straight pin or toothpick.

11. Dry flat for 4 to 6 hours. The paint will cure completely in 24 hours and the shirt can be washed after 72 hours. To launder, turn the shirt inside out and wash in warm water on delicate cycle. Tumble dry on low heat.

How does your

garden grow?

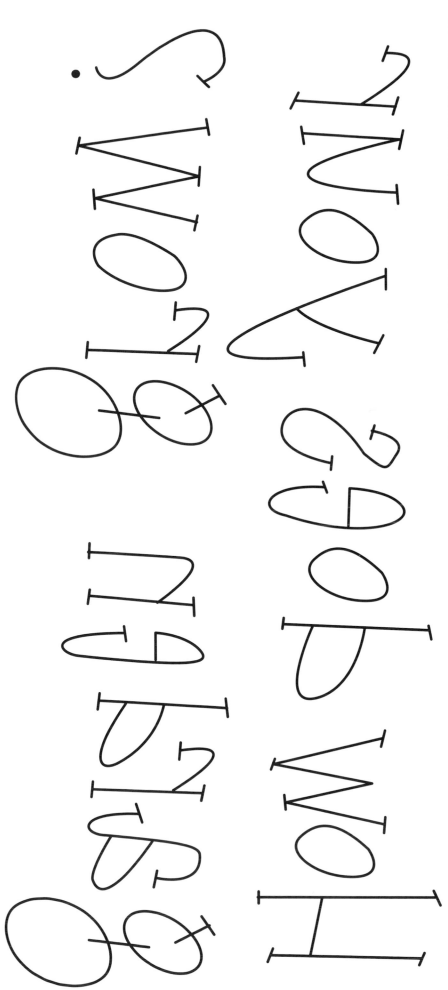

Reproduce pattern
pieces at 100%.

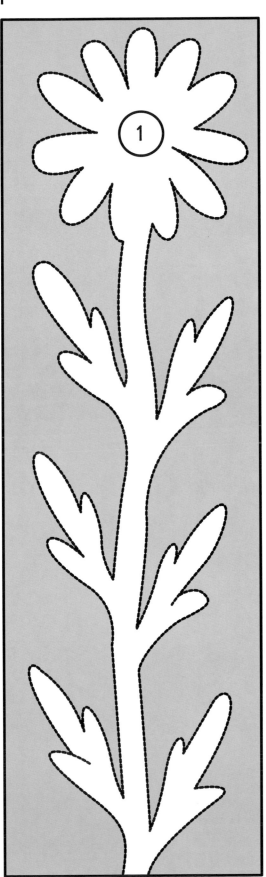

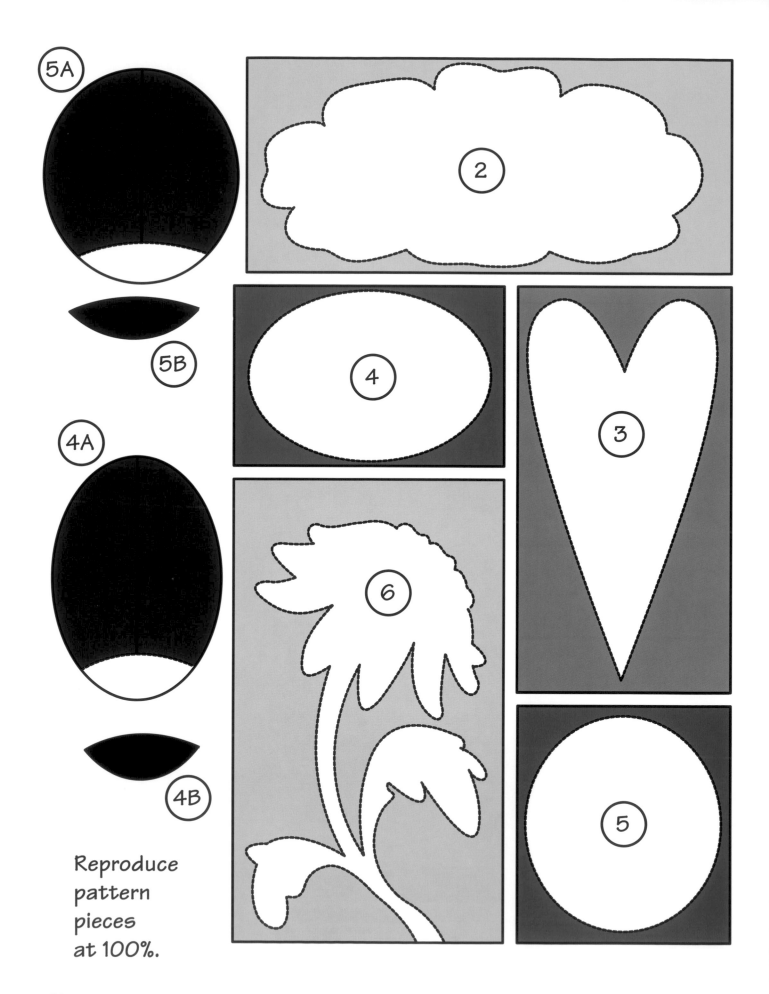

5A

2

5B

4

3

4A

6

4B

5

Reproduce
pattern
pieces
at 100%.

62

Reproduce
pattern
pieces
at 100%.

Under the sea ...

Materials

100% cotton sheeting shirt
Fusing adhesive, ³/₈ yard
Fabric writer, gold
Pencil or non-permanent pen
Scissors
Tape measure
Iron
Straight pin or toothpick

Fabrics for pattern pieces

By Name	By Number/Letter	Size
Background	1	8" x 12"
Fish	2	5" x 5"
Fish Tail & Eye Piece	2A and 2B	5" x 9"
Eyeball & Bubbles	2C, 5	5" x 5"
Fins	3A and 3B	4" x 4"
Lips	2E	2" x 2"
Seaweed	4A and 4B	5" x 5"
Eye	2D	Scrap

Instructions

1. Pre-wash the shirt and all the appliqué fabrics to remove sizing and reduce shrinkage. Do not use fabric softener.

2. All the patterns in this book are the reverse of how they will appear on the shirt. Lay the fusing adhesive, paper side up, onto the patterns from pages 67-69 (after they have been enlarged 117%) and trace. The broken lines are positioning and/or painting lines.

3. Cut the shapes that you have traced onto the fusing adhesive apart and fuse, according to manufacturer's instructions, to the wrong sides of the appliqué fabrics. Let all fabrics cool. Do not remove paper backing yet.

4. Cut all fabric shapes out along traced pencil lines. Remove paper backing.

5. Using a pencil or non-permanent pen, transfer pattern markings and details for painting. For example: the lines on the fins and the reflections in the bubbles.

6. Find the center of the shirt by folding it in half down the center front. Press a slight crease to mark the center.

7. Position the background (1) on the shirt front. Fold this piece in half, matching the long sides, and make a crease in the top and bottom with your fingers. Match this crease with the crease on the front of the shirt to center the design. Piece 1 should be placed about 3" down from the neckline. Fuse piece 1 in place according to manufacturer's instructions.

8. Referring to the photograph, position the remaining pieces on the shirt, in the following order: Fish (2), Fish Tail (2A), Eyeball (2C), Eye Piece (2B), Eye (2D), Fins (3A, 3B), Seaweed (4A, 4B), and Bubbles (5). Cut as many bubbles as desired and place them randomly on the shirt. Fuse all pieces at once according to manufacturer's instructions.

9. Using a gold fabric writer, outline the raw edges of all the appliqué pieces, beginning at the upper left-hand side if you are right-handed or at the upper right-hand side if you are left-handed. You may also choose to embellish with additional painted lines. Use a steady hand and constant pressure on the bottle—any stray paint splatters can easily be removed with a straight pin or toothpick.

10. Dry flat for 4 to 6 hours. The paint will cure completely in 24 hours and the shirt can be washed after 72 hours. To launder, turn the shirt inside out and wash in warm water on delicate cycle. Tumble dry on low heat.

Reproduce pattern
pieces at 117%.

Reproduce pattern
pieces at 117%.

2A

5

5

5

5

4A

2D

2B

2C

4B

Reproduce pattern
pieces at 117%.

69

Talk to the animals ...

Materials

100% cotton sheeting shirt
Fusing adhesive, 1/2 yard
Fabric writer, black
Pencil or non-permanent pen
Scissors
Tape measure
Iron
Straight pin or toothpick

Fabrics for pattern pieces

By Name	By Number/Letter	Size
Background	1	4" x 12"
Background	2	3" x 4"
Background	3	4" x 4"
Background, Bear's Face, Giraffe's Spots & Monkey's Muzzle	4, 3A, 1B, 6B	7" x 8"
Background	5	3" x 5"
Giraffe, Lion, Pelican's Beak & Background	1A, 4A, 5B, 6	6" x 12"
Bunny & Lion's Eyes	2A, 4C	3" x 5"
Bear's Muzzle, Bear's Ears & Lion's Face	3B, 3C, 4B	4" x 5"
Pelican	5A	3" x 3"
Monkey	6A	4" x 5"

Instructions

1. Pre-wash the shirt and all the appliqué fabrics to remove sizing and reduce shrinkage. Do not use fabric softener.

2. All the patterns in this book are the reverse of how they will appear on the shirt. Lay the fusing adhesive, paper side up, onto the patterns from pages 73-75 (after they have been enlarged 125%) and trace. The broken lines are positioning and/or painting lines.

3. Cut the shapes that you have traced onto the fusing adhesive apart and fuse, according to manufacturer's instructions, to the wrong sides of the appliqué fabrics. Let all fabrics cool. Do not remove paper backing yet.

4. Cut all fabric shapes out along traced pencil lines. Remove paper backing.

5. Using a pencil or non-permanent pen, transfer pattern markings and details for painting. For example: all animal details, faces, etc.

6. Find the center of the shirt by folding it in half down the center front. Press a slight crease to mark the center.

7. Fold piece 2 in half, matching the long sides, and make a crease in the top and bottom with your fingers. Match this crease with the crease on the front of the shirt to center the design. Piece 2 should be placed about 3" down from the neckline. Fuse piece 2 in place according to manufacturer's instructions. Position all other background pieces (1, 3, 4, 5, 6) around piece 2 parallel with the crease.

8. Referring to the photograph, position the remaining pieces on the shirt, in the following order: Giraffe (1A), Giraffe's Spots (1B), Bunny (2A), Bear's Face (3A), Bear's Muzzle (3B), Bear's Ears (3C), Lion (4A), Lion's Face (4B), Lion's Eyes (4C), Pelican (5A), Pelican's Beak (5B), Monkey (6A), and Monkey's Muzzle (6B). Fuse all pieces at once according to manufacturer's instructions.

9. Using a black fabric writer, outline the raw edges of all the appliqué pieces, beginning at the upper left-hand side if you are right-handed or at the upper right-hand side if you are left-handed. You may also choose to embellish with additional painted lines. Use a steady hand and constant pressure on the bottle—any stray paint splatters can easily be removed with a straight pin or toothpick.

10. Dry flat for 4 to 6 hours. The paint will cure completely in 24 hours and the shirt can be washed after 72 hours. To launder, turn the shirt inside out and wash in warm water on delicate cycle. Tumble dry on low heat.

Reproduce pattern
pieces at 125%.

Reproduce pattern
pieces at 125%.

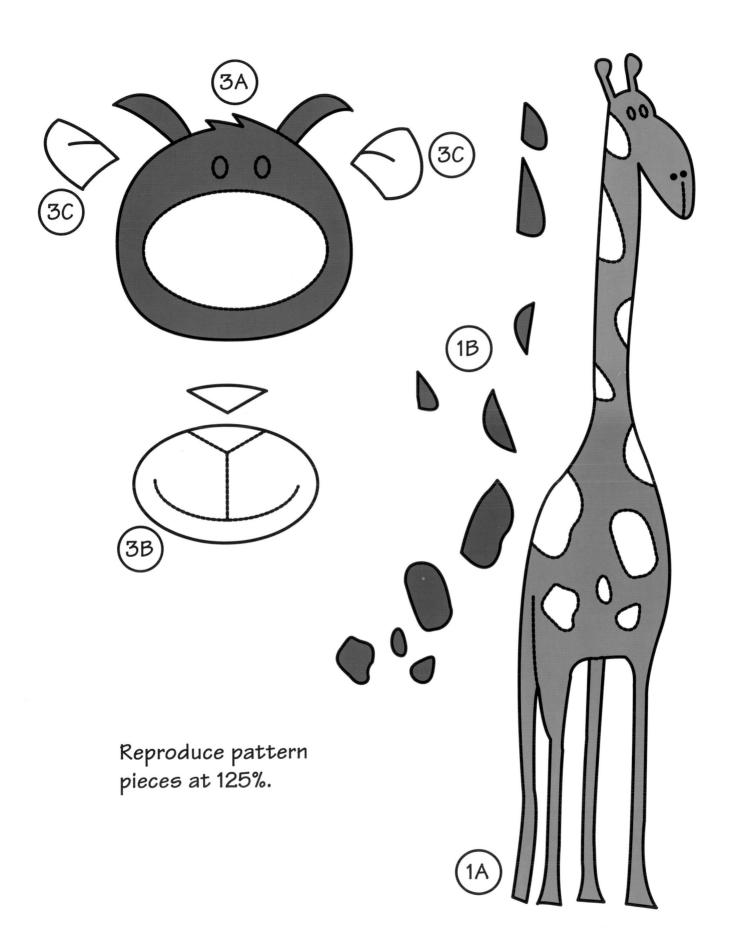

3A

3C

3C

3B

1B

1A

Reproduce pattern
pieces at 125%.

Smiling sunflowers ...

Materials

100% cotton sheeting shirt
Fusing adhesive, ³/₈ yard
Fabric writer, black
Pencil or non-permanent pen
Scissors
Tape measure
Iron
Straight pin or toothpick

Fabrics for pattern pieces

By Name	By Number/Letter	Size
Background	1	8" x 11"
Sunflowers	2	11" x 12"
Faces	3, 4, 5	6" x 7"
Eyes	3A, 4A, 5A	2" x 2"
Foliage	3B, 4B, 5B	6" x 6"

Instructions

1. Pre-wash the shirt and all the appliqué fabrics to remove sizing and reduce shrinkage. Do not use fabric softener.

2. All the patterns in this book are the reverse of how they will appear on the shirt. Lay the fusing adhesive, paper side up, onto the patterns from pages 79-81 (after they have been enlarged 142%) and trace. The broken lines are positioning and/or painting lines.

3. Cut the shapes that you have traced onto the fusing adhesive apart and fuse, according to manufacturer's instructions, to the wrong sides of the appliqué fabrics. Let all fabrics cool. Do not remove paper backing yet.

4. Cut all fabric shapes out along traced pencil lines. Remove paper backing.

5. Using a pencil or non-permanent pen, transfer pattern markings and details for painting. For example: flower petal lines, smiles, and foliage details.

6. Find the center of the shirt by folding it in half down the center front. Press a slight crease to mark the center.

7. Position the background (1) on the shirt front. Fold this piece in half, matching the long sides, and make a crease in the top and bottom with your fingers. Match this crease with the crease on the front of the shirt to center the design. Piece 1 should be placed about 3" down from the neckline. Fuse piece 1 in place according to manufacturer's instructions.

8. Referring to the photograph, position the remaining pieces on the shirt, in the following order: Sunflowers (2), Faces (3, 4, 5), Eyes and Foliage (3A, 3B), Eyes and Foliage (4A, 4B), and Eyes and Foliage (5A, 5B). Fuse all pieces at once according to manufacturer's instructions.

9. Using a black fabric writer, outline the raw edges of all the appliqué pieces, beginning at the upper left-hand side if you are right-handed or at the upper right-hand side if you are left-handed. You may also choose to embellish with additional painted lines. Use a steady hand and constant pressure on the bottle—any stray paint splatters can easily be removed with a straight pin or toothpick.

10. Dry flat for 4 to 6 hours. The paint will cure completely in 24 hours and the shirt can be washed after 72 hours. To launder, turn the shirt inside out and wash in warm water on delicate cycle. Tumble dry on low heat.

Reproduce pattern
pieces at 142%.

Reproduce pattern
pieces at 142%.

Reproduce pattern
pieces at 142%.

The cow jumped over the moon ...

Materials

- Sweatshirt
- Fusing adhesive, ³/₈ yard
- Fabric writer, black
- Pencil or non-permanent pen
- Scissors
- Tape measure
- Iron
- Straight pin or toothpick

Fabrics for pattern pieces

By Name	By Number/Letter	Size
Background	1	9" x 11"
Cow	2	7" x 11"
Cow's Spots & Hooves	2A thru 2G	6" x 6"
Cow's Eyes	2H	Scrap
Cow's Udder & Inner Ears	2I and 2J	2" x 2"
Moon	3	4" x 5"
Stars	4A thru 4C	6" x 6"

Instructions

1. Pre-wash the sweatshirt and all the appliqué fabrics to remove sizing and reduce shrinkage. Do not use fabric softener.

2. All the patterns in this book are the reverse of how they will appear on the sweatshirt. Lay the fusing adhesive, paper side up, onto the patterns from pages 85-87 (after they have been enlarged 117%) and trace. The broken lines are positioning and/or painting lines.

3. Cut the shapes that you have traced onto the fusing adhesive apart and fuse, according to manufacturer's instructions, to the wrong sides of the appliqué fabrics. Let all fabrics cool. Do not remove paper backing yet.

4. Cut all fabric shapes out along traced pencil lines. Remove paper backing.

5. Using a pencil or non-permanent pen, transfer pattern markings and details for painting. For example: cow's details and moon's facial details.

6. Find the center of the sweatshirt by folding it in half down the center front. Press a slight crease to mark the center.

7. Position the background (1) on the sweatshirt front. Fold this piece in half, matching the long sides, and make a crease in the top and bottom with your fingers. Match this crease with the crease on the front of the sweatshirt to center the design. Piece 1 should be placed about 3" down from the neckline. Fuse piece 1 in place according to manufacturer's instructions.

8. Referring to the photograph, position the remaining pieces on the sweatshirt, in the following order: Cow (2), Cow's Spots and Hooves (2A, 2B, 2C, 2D, 2E, 2F, 2G), Cow's Eyes (2H), Cow's Udder and Inner Ears (2I, 2J), Moon (3), and Stars (4A, 4B, 4C). Fuse all pieces at once according to manufacturer's instructions.

9. Using a black fabric writer, outline the raw edges of all the appliqué pieces, beginning at the upper left-hand side if you are right-handed or at the upper right-hand side if you are left-handed. You may also choose to embellish with additional painted lines. Use a steady hand and constant pressure on the bottle—any stray paint splatters can easily be removed with a straight pin or toothpick.

10. Dry flat for 4 to 6 hours. The paint will cure completely in 24 hours and the sweatshirt can be washed after 72 hours. To launder, turn the sweatshirt inside out and wash in warm water on delicate cycle. Tumble-dry on low heat.

1

Reproduce pattern
pieces at 117%.

Reproduce pattern
pieces at 117%.

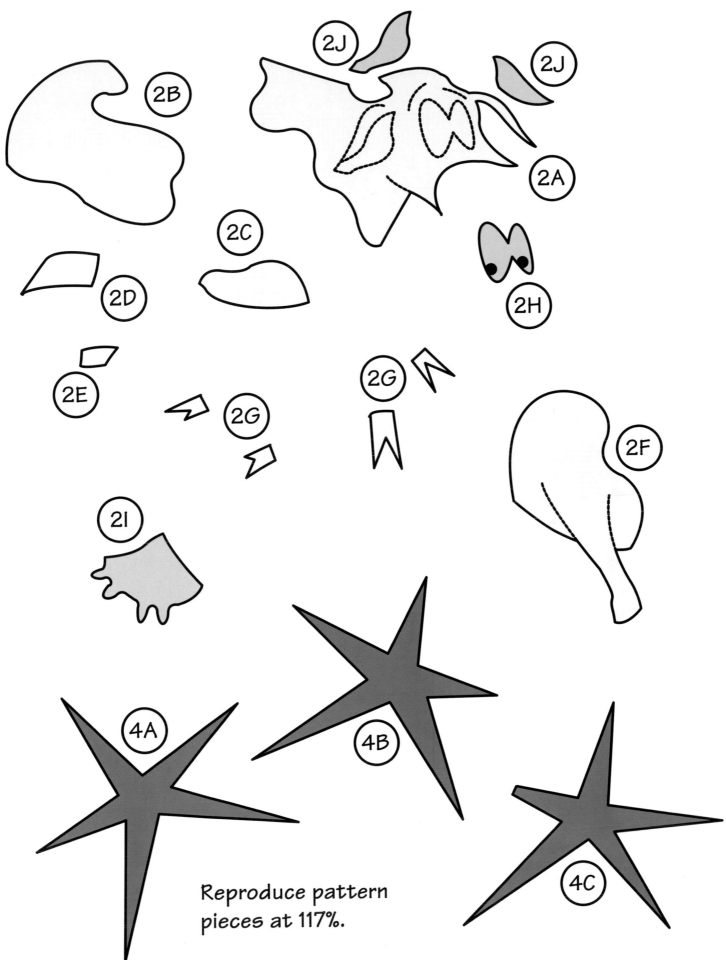

Reproduce pattern
pieces at 117%.

Bear necessity ...

Materials

100% cotton sheeting shirt
Fusing adhesive, ³⁄₈ yard
Fabric writer, black
Pencil or non-permanent pen
Scissors
Tape measure
Iron
Straight pin or toothpick
2 black buttons
Coordinating thread

Fabrics for pattern pieces

By Name	By Number/Letter	Size
Background	1	7" x 10"
Teddy Bear	2	9" x 10"
Belly, Muzzle, Inner Ears & Arms & Legs	2A, 2B, 2D, 2F	6" x 6"
Nose	2C	2" x 2"
Bow	3	3" x 4"
Patch	2E	2" x 2"

Instructions

1. Pre-wash the shirt and all the appliqué fabrics to remove sizing and reduce shrinkage. Do not use fabric softener.

2. All the patterns in this book are the reverse of how they will appear on the shirt. Lay the fusing adhesive, paper side up, onto the patterns from pages 91-93 (after they have been enlarged 111%) and trace. The broken lines are positioning and/or painting lines.

3. Cut the shapes that you have traced onto the fusing adhesive apart and fuse, according to manufacturer's instructions, to the wrong sides of the appliqué fabrics. Let all fabrics cool. Do not remove paper backing yet.

4. Cut all fabric shapes out along traced pencil lines. Remove paper backing.

5. Using a pencil or non-permanent pen, transfer pattern markings and details for painting. For example: mouth, detail on the bow, "stitching," and the button placement for the eyes.

6. Find the center of the shirt by folding it in half down the center front. Press a slight crease to mark the center.

7. Position the background (1) on the shirt front. Fold this piece in half, matching the long sides, and make a crease in the top and bottom with your fingers. Match this crease with the crease on the front of the shirt to center the design. Piece 1 should be placed about 3" down from the neckline. Fuse piece 1 in place according to manufacturer's instructions.

8. Referring to the photograph, position the remaining pieces on the shirt, in the following order: Teddy Bear (2), Belly (2A), Muzzle (2B), Nose (2C), Inner Ears (2D), Patch (2E), Arms and Legs (2F), and Bow (3). Fuse all pieces at once according to manufacturer's instructions.

9. Using a black fabric writer, outline the raw edges of all the appliqué pieces, beginning at the upper left-hand side if you are right-handed or at the upper right-hand side if you are left-handed. You may also choose to embellish with additional painted lines. Use a steady hand and constant pressure on the bottle—any stray paint splatters can easily be removed with a straight pin or toothpick.

10. Using coordinating thread, stitch the buttons for the eyes where marked after the paint has dried.

11. Dry flat for 4 to 6 hours. The paint will cure completely in 24 hours and the shirt can be washed after 72 hours. To launder, turn the shirt inside out and wash in warm water on delicate cycle. Tumble dry on low heat.

Reproduce pattern
pieces at 111%.

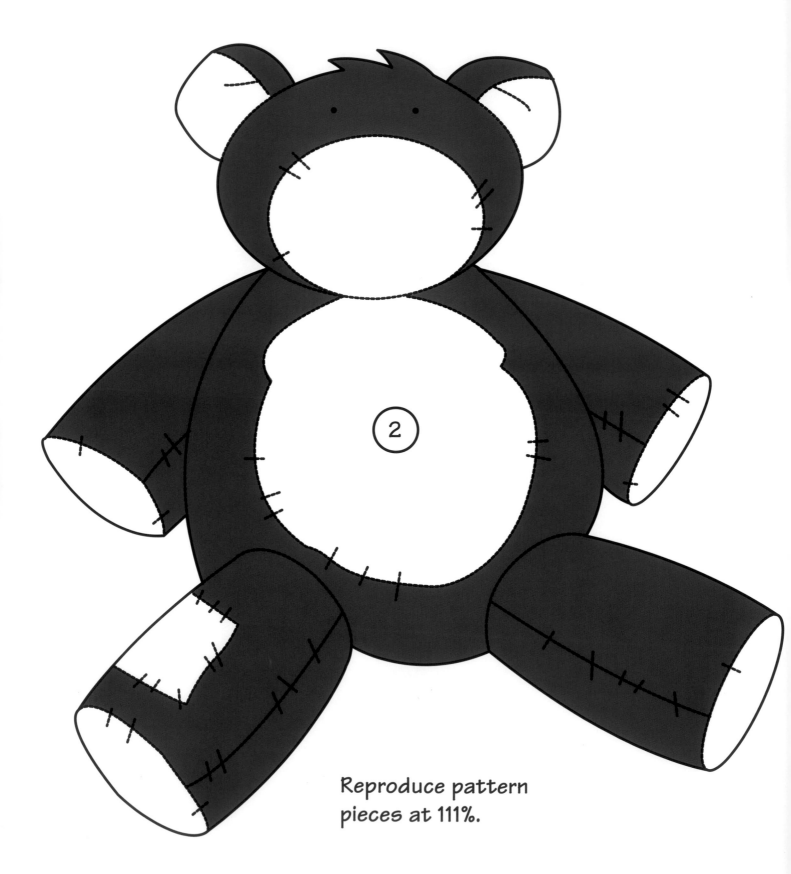

Reproduce pattern
pieces at 111%.

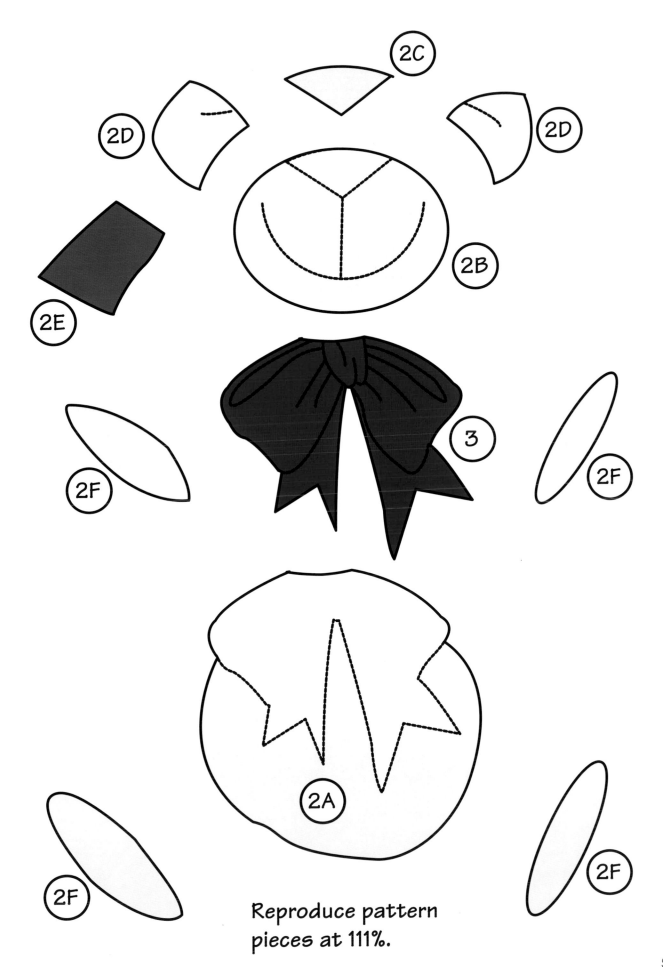

Reproduce pattern pieces at 111%.

Sail into summer ...

Materials

100% cotton sheeting shirt
Fusing adhesive, $^3/_8$ yard
Fabric writer, gold
Pencil or non-permanent pen
Scissors
Tape measure
Iron
Straight pin or toothpick

Fabrics for pattern pieces

By Name	By Number/Letter	Size
Background	1	7" x 12"
Sun & Rays (cut 8)	2, 2A	5" x 5"
Sails & Boat	3, 5	7" x 10"
Stripe	3A	3" x 3"
Stripe	3B	3" x 3"
Water	6	3" x 7"
Clouds	4A and 4B	4" x 4"

Instructions

1. Pre-wash the shirt and all the appliqué fabrics to remove sizing and reduce shrinkage. Do not use fabric softener.

2. All the patterns in this book are the reverse of how they will appear on the shirt. Lay the fusing adhesive, paper side up, onto the patterns from pages 97-99 (after they have been enlarged 117%) and trace. The broken lines are positioning and/or painting lines.

3. Cut the shapes that you have traced onto the fusing adhesive apart and fuse, according to manufacturer's instructions, to the wrong sides of the appliqué fabrics. Let all fabrics cool. Do not remove paper backing yet.

4. Cut all fabric shapes out along traced pencil lines. Remove paper backing.

5. Find the center of the shirt by folding it in half down the center front. Press a slight crease to mark the center.

6. Position the background (1) on the shirt front. Fold this piece in half, matching the long sides, and make a crease in the top and bottom with your fingers. Match this crease with the crease on the front of the shirt to center the design. Piece 1 should be placed about 3" down from the neckline. Fuse piece 1 in place according to manufacturer's instructions.

7. Referring to the photograph, position the remaining pieces on the shirt, in the following order: Sun (2), Rays (2A), Sails (3), Stripe (3A), Stripe (3B), Clouds (4A, 4B), Boat (5), and Water (6). If your sail fabric is lighter in color than your ray fabric, draw a line with a pencil where the sail meets the rays and cut the section that falls underneath the sail away. Slip the ray pieces under the sail $^1/_8$". Fuse all pieces at once according to manufacturer's instructions.

8. Using a gold fabric writer, outline the raw edges of all the appliqué pieces, beginning at the upper left-hand side if you are right-handed or at the upper right-hand side if you are left-handed. You may also choose to embellish with additional painted lines. Use a steady hand and constant pressure on the bottle—any stray paint splatters can easily be removed with a straight pin or toothpick.

9. Dry flat for 4 to 6 hours. The paint will cure completely in 24 hours and the shirt can be washed after 72 hours. To launder, turn the shirt inside out and wash in warm water on delicate cycle. Tumble dry on low heat.

Reproduce pattern
pieces at 117%.

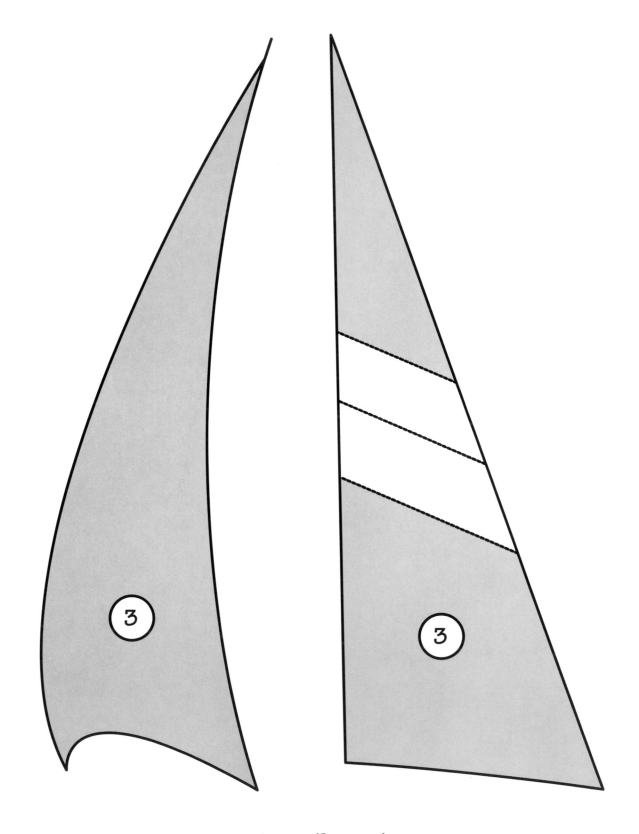

Reproduce pattern
pieces at 117%.

Reproduce pattern
pieces at 117%.

Stars & swirls ...

Materials

- Sweatshirt
- Fusing adhesive, 3/8 yard
- Fabric writer, gold
- Pencil or non-permanent pen
- Scissors
- Tape measure
- Iron
- Straight pin or toothpick

Fabrics for pattern pieces

By Name	By Number/Letter	Size
Large Swirls	1	8" x 8"
Small Swirls	2	5" x 5"
Stars	3	8" x 8"

Instructions

1. Pre-wash the sweatshirt and all the appliqué fabrics to remove sizing and reduce shrinkage. Do not use fabric softener.

2. All the patterns in this book are the reverse of how they will appear on the sweatshirt. Lay the fusing adhesive, paper side up, onto the patterns on pages 102-103 and trace. The broken lines are positioning and/or painting lines.

3. Cut the shapes that you have traced onto the fusing adhesive apart and fuse, according to manufacturer's instructions, to the wrong sides of the appliqué fabrics. Let all fabrics cool. Do not remove paper backing yet.

4. Cut all fabric shapes out along traced pencil lines. Remove paper backing.

5. Position the Stars (3) and Swirls (1, 2) randomly on the front of the sweatshirt. Note that the amount of fabric used for the appliqué pattern pieces depends on the number of shapes you plan to use. Fuse all pieces at once according to manu-facturer's instructions.

6. Using a gold fabric writer, outline the raw edges of all the appliqué pieces. You may also choose to embellish with additional painted lines. Use a steady hand and constant pressure on the bottle—any stray paint splatters can easily be removed with a straight pin or toothpick.

7. Dry flat for 4 to 6 hours. The paint will cure completely in 24 hours and the sweatshirt can be washed after 72 hours. To launder, turn the sweatshirt inside out and wash in warm water on delicate cycle. Tumble-dry on low heat.

Reproduce pattern
pieces at 100%.

Reproduce pattern pieces at 100%.

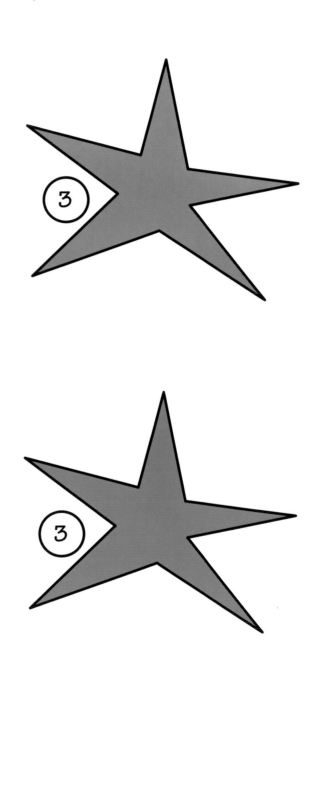

Teacher's pet ...

Materials

- Sweatshirt
- Fusing adhesive, ³/₈ yard
- Fabric writer, black
- Fabric writer, gold
- Pencil or non-permanent pen
- Scissors
- Tape measure
- Iron
- Straight pin or toothpick

Fabrics for pattern pieces

By Name	By Number/Letter	Size
Background	1	6" x 8"
Pencils (cut 2 each size)	2	6" x 10"
Pencil Wood (cut 4)	2A	3" x 4"
Pencil Erasers (cut 4)	2B	2" x 2"
Apple	3A	6" x 7"
Apple Stem	3B	2" x 2"
Heart	4	5" x 5"

Instructions

1. Pre-wash the sweatshirt and all the appliqué fabrics to remove sizing and reduce shrinkage. Do not use fabric softener.

2. All the patterns in this book are the reverse of how they will appear on the sweatshirt. Lay the fusing adhesive, paper side up, onto the patterns on pages 107-109 and trace. The broken lines are positioning and/or painting lines.

3. Cut the shapes that you have traced onto the fusing adhesive apart and fuse, according to manufacturer's instructions, to the wrong sides of the appliqué fabrics. Let all fabrics cool. Do not remove paper backing yet.

4. Cut all fabric shapes out along traced pencil lines. Remove paper backing.

5. Using a pencil or non-permanent pen, transfer pattern markings and details for painting. For example: pencil details and stem detail.

6. Find the center of the sweatshirt by folding it in half down the center front. Press a slight crease to mark the center.

7. Position the background (1) on the sweatshirt front. Fold this piece in half, matching the long sides, and make a crease in the top and bottom with your fingers. Match this crease with the crease on the front of the sweatshirt to center the design. Piece 1 should be placed about 3" down from the neckline.

Fuse piece 1 in place according to manufacturer's instructions.

8. Referring to the photograph, position the remaining pieces on the sweatshirt, in the following order: Pencils (2), Pencil Wood (2A), Pencil Erasers (2B), Apple (3A), Apple Stem (3B), and Heart (4). Fuse all pieces at once according to manufacturer's instructions.

9. Using a gold fabric writer, outline the raw edges of all the appliqué pieces, beginning at the upper left-hand side if you are right-handed or at the upper right-hand side if you are left-handed. Continue down the front of the sweatshirt with the gold fabric writer until you get to the pencil lead. Using a black fabric writer, paint the pencil lead. Using the gold fabric writer, finish painting the design. You may also choose to embellish with additional painted lines. Use a steady hand and constant pressure on the bottle—any stray paint splatters can easily be removed with a straight pin or toothpick.

10. Dry flat for 4 to 6 hours. The paint will cure completely in 24 hours and the sweatshirt can be washed after 72 hours. To launder, turn the sweatshirt inside out and wash in warm water on delicate cycle. Tumble-dry on low heat.

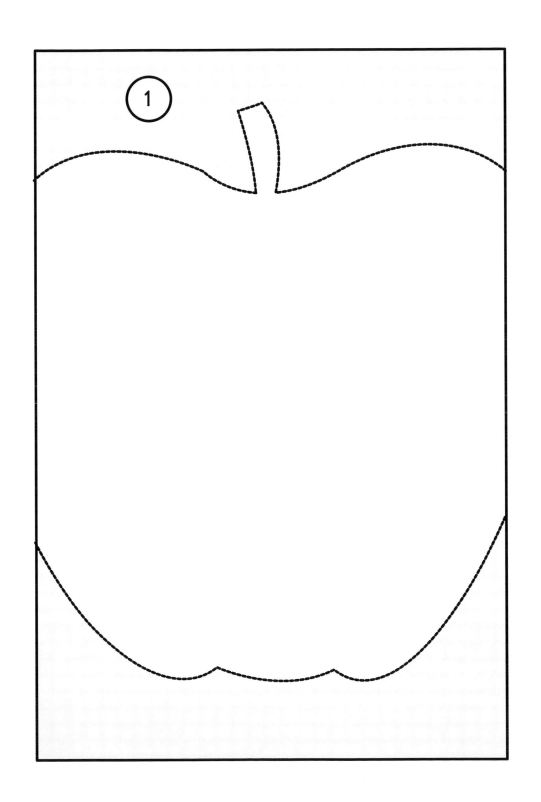

Reproduce pattern
pieces at 100%.

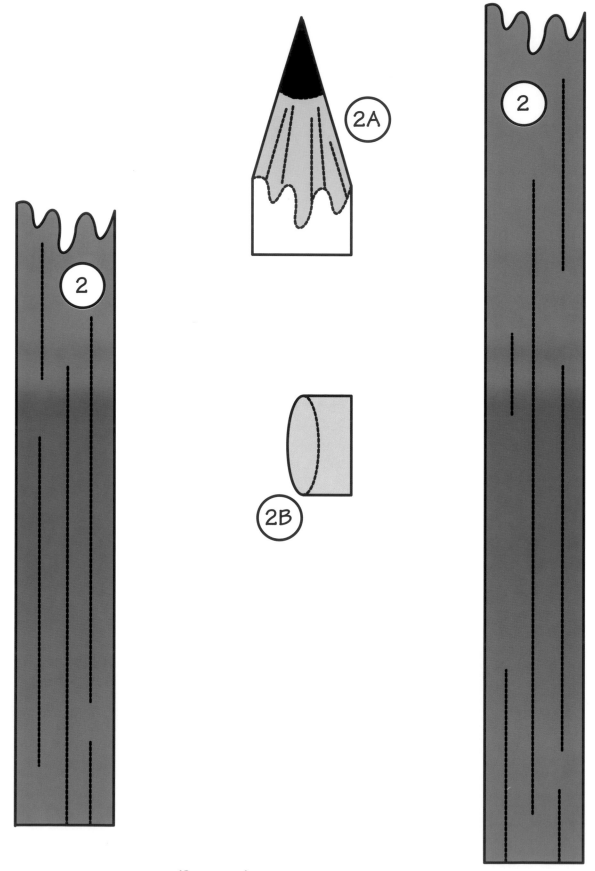

Reproduce pattern
pieces at 100%.

x

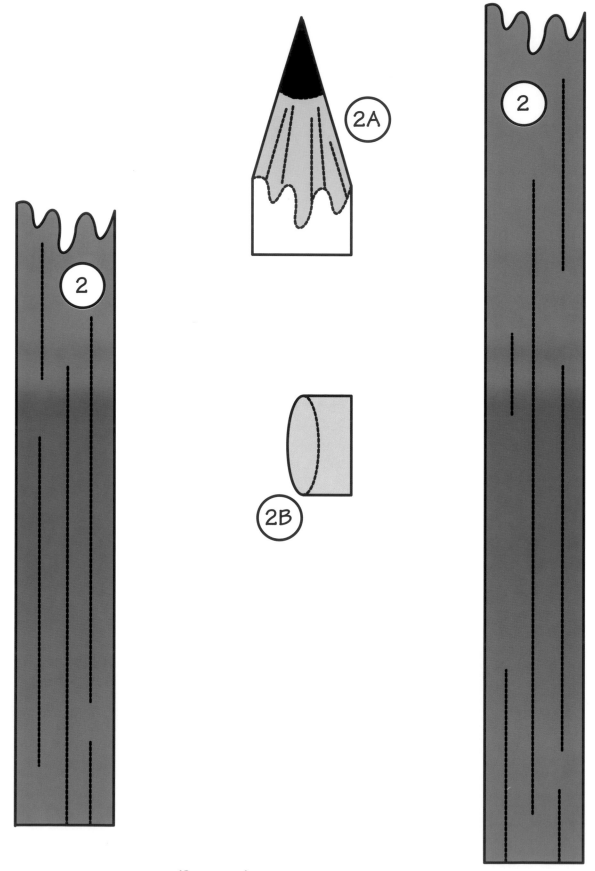

Reproduce pattern
pieces at 100%.

Reproduce pattern
pieces at 100%.

Silly scarecrow ...

Materials

100% cotton sheeting shirt
Fusing adhesive, 1/2 yard
Fabric writer, black
Pencil or non-permanent pen
Scissors
Tape measure
Iron
Straight pin or toothpick

Fabrics for pattern pieces

By Name	By Number/Letter	Size
Background	1	8" x 13"
Scarecrow Face & Hood	2	9" x 11"
Eyes	2A and 2B	3" x 3"
Nose	2C	3" x 3"
Cheeks	2D	3" x 3"
Hat	3	8" x 10"
Patch	3A	2" x 2"
Straw Hair	3B	5" x 5"
Neck	2E	2" x 3"

Instructions

1. Pre-wash the shirt and all the appliqué fabrics to remove sizing and reduce shrinkage. Do not use fabric softener.

2. All the patterns in this book are the reverse of how they will appear on the shirt. Lay the fusing adhesive, paper side up, onto the patterns from pages 113-115 (after they have been enlarged 125%) and trace. The broken lines are positioning and/or painting lines.

3. Cut the shapes that you have traced onto the fusing adhesive apart and fuse, according to manufacturer's instructions, to the wrong sides of the appliqué fabrics. Let all fabrics cool. Do not remove paper backing yet.

4. Cut all fabric shapes out along traced pencil lines. Remove paper backing.

5. Using a pencil or non-permanent pen, transfer pattern markings and details for painting. For example: the scarecrow's mouth, stitching lines on the patch, and the fold lines on the hood.

6. Find the center of the shirt by folding it in half down the center front. Press a slight crease to mark the center.

7. Position the background (1) on the shirt front. Fold this piece in half, matching the long sides, and make a crease in the top and bottom with your fingers. Match this crease with the crease on the front of the shirt to center the design. Piece 1 should be placed about 3" down from the neckline. Fuse piece 1 in place according to manufacturer's instructions.

8. Referring to the photograph, position the remaining pieces on the shirt, in the following order: Scarecrow Face & Hood (2), Hat (3), Patch (3A), Straw Hair (3B), Nose (2C), Eyes (2A, 2B), Cheeks (2D), and Neck (2E). Fuse all pieces at once according to manufacturer's instructions.

9. Using a black fabric writer, outline the raw edges of all the appliqué pieces, beginning at the upper left-hand side if you are right-handed or at the upper right-hand side if you are left-handed. You may also choose to embellish with additional painted lines. Use a steady hand and constant pressure on the bottle—any stray paint splatters can easily be removed with a straight pin or toothpick.

10. Dry flat for 4 to 6 hours. The paint will cure completely in 24 hours and the shirt can be washed after 72 hours. To launder, turn the shirt inside out and wash in warm water on delicate cycle. Tumble dry on low heat.

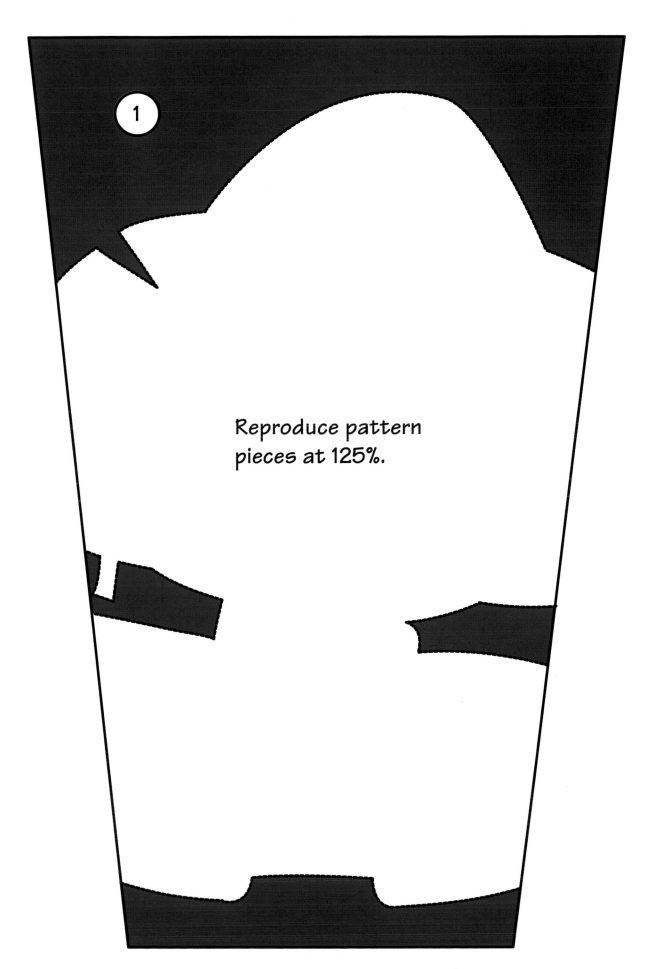

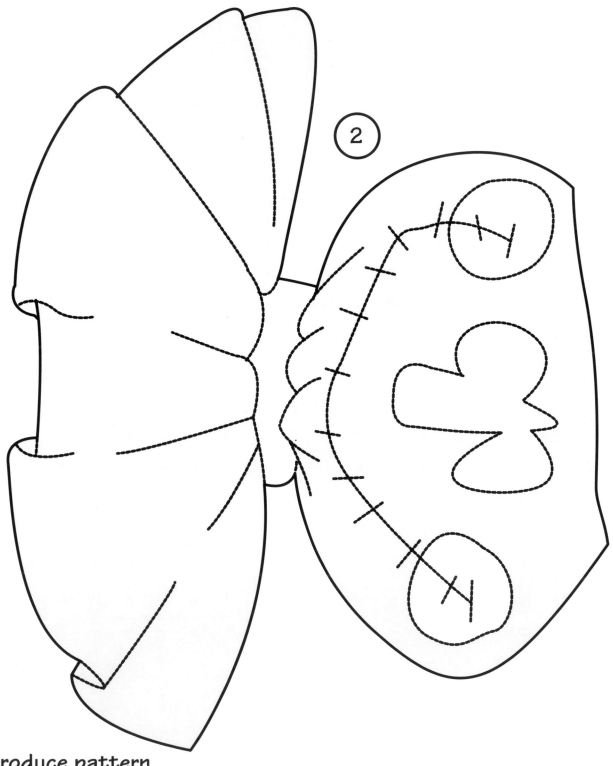

Reproduce pattern
pieces at 125%.

Reproduce pattern
pieces at 125%.

Happy Halloween ...

Materials

100% cotton sheeting shirt
Fusing adhesive, 1/3 yard
Fabric writer, gold
Pencil or non-permanent pen
Scissors
Tape measure
Straight pin
Iron
Tracing paper
Straight pin or toothpick
Iron-on transfer pencil

Fabrics for pattern pieces

By Name	By Number/Letter	Size
Pumpkin	1	6" x 10"
Eyes, Nose,	1A thru 1C,	
Mouth & Stars	3A thru 3C	8" x 8"
Stem	2	2" x 2"
Moon	4	3" x 4"

Instructions

1. Pre-wash the shirt and all the appliqué fabrics to remove sizing and reduce shrinkage. Do not use fabric softener.

2. All the patterns in this book are the reverse of how they will appear on the shirt. Lay the fusing adhesive, paper side up, onto the patterns on pages 119-121 and trace. The broken lines are positioning and/or painting lines.

3. Cut the shapes that you have traced onto the fusing adhesive apart and fuse, according to manufacturer's instructions, to the wrong sides of the appliqué fabrics. Let all fabrics cool. Do not remove paper backing yet.

4. Cut all fabric shapes out along traced pencil lines. Remove paper backing.

5. Using a pencil or non-permanent pen, transfer pattern markings and details for painting. For example: pumpkin detail, mouth, "stitching," and lettering.

6. Find the center of the shirt by folding it in half down the center front. Press a slight crease to mark the center.

7. Measure 3" down from the neckline on the centerline of the shirt. Mark that measurement with a straight pin. This will be the position of the piece that is closest to the neckline.

8. Referring to the photograph, position the pieces on the shirt, in the following order: Pumpkin (1), Eyes (1A), Nose (1B), Mouth (1C), Stem (2), Stars (3A, 3B, 3C), and Moon (4). Fuse all pieces at once according to manufacturer's instructions.

9. Transfer the lettering to your shirt by laying the piece of tracing paper over the lettering pattern and trace over it with an iron-on transfer pencil. Turn the traced pattern, transfer pencil side down, on your shirt and press it on using a warm iron.

10. Using a gold fabric writer, outline the raw edges of all the appliqué pieces, beginning at the upper left-hand side if you are right-handed or at the upper right-hand side if you are left-handed. You may also choose to embellish with additional painted lines. Use a steady hand and constant pressure on the bottle—any stray paint splatters can easily be removed with a straight pin or toothpick.

11. Dry flat for 4 to 6 hours. The paint will cure completely in 24 hours and the shirt can be washed after 72 hours. To launder, turn the shirt inside out and wash in warm water on delicate cycle. Tumble dry on low heat.

Happy Halloween

Happy Halloween

Reproduce pattern
pieces at 100%.

Reproduce pattern
pieces at 100%.

Reproduce pattern
pieces at 100%.

Christmas baubles ...

Materials

100% cotton sheeting shirt
Fusing adhesive, $^3/_8$ yard
Fabric writer, gold
Rhinestones, asst. sizes/colors
Pencil or non-permanent pen
Scissors
Tape measure
Iron
Straight pin or toothpick

Fabrics for pattern pieces

By Name	By Number/Letter	Size
Backgrounds & Ornament	1, 4, 2A	9" x 9"
Backgrounds & Ornament	2, 3, 4A	9" x 9"
Ornament & Decoration	3A, 2C thru 2E	5" x 5"
Ornament	1A	4" x 4"
Decoration	3C	2" x 3"
Hangers &	1B, 2B, 3B, 4B,	
Decorations	1C, 4C	4" x 5"

Instructions

1. Pre-wash the shirt and all the appliqué fabrics to remove sizing and reduce shrinkage. Do not use fabric softener.

2. All the patterns in this book are the reverse of how they will appear on the shirt. Lay the fusing adhesive, paper side up, onto the patterns from pages 125-127 (after they have been enlarged 117%) and trace. The broken lines are positioning and/or painting lines.

3. Cut the shapes that you have traced onto the fusing adhesive apart and fuse, according to manufacturer's instructions, to the wrong sides of the appliqué fabrics. Let all fabrics cool. Do not remove paper backing yet.

4. Cut all fabric shapes out along traced pencil lines. Remove paper backing.

5. Using a pencil or non-permanent pen, transfer pattern markings and details for painting.

6. Find the center of the shirt by folding it in half down the center front. Press a slight crease to mark the center.

7. Position the backgrounds (1, 2, 3, 4) on the shirt front. Match these pieces with the crease on the front of the shirt to center the design. Pieces 1-4 should be placed about 3" down from the neckline. Fuse these pieces in place according to manu-

facturer's instructions.

8. Referring to the photograph, position the remaining pieces on the shirt, in the following order: Ornament (1A), Hanger (1B), Decoration (1C), Ornament (2A), Hanger (2B), Decorations (2C, 2D, 2E), Ornament (3A), Hanger (3B), Decoration (3C), Ornament (4A), Hanger (4B), and Decoration (4C). Fuse all pieces at once according to manufacturer's instructions.

9. Using a gold fabric writer, outline the raw edges of all the appliqué pieces, beginning at the upper left-hand side if you are right-handed or at the upper right-hand side if you are left-handed. As you go, scatter the rhinestones and set each one in place by using a thick dot of paint and sinking each rhinestone into the center of each paint dot. Push the rhinestone down gently. You may also choose to embellish with additional painted lines. Use a steady hand and constant pressure on the bottle—any stray paint splatters can easily be removed with a straight pin or toothpick.

10. Dry flat for 4 to 6 hours. The paint will cure completely in 24 hours and the shirt can be washed after 72 hours. To launder, turn the shirt inside out and wash in warm water on delicate cycle. Tumble dry on low heat.

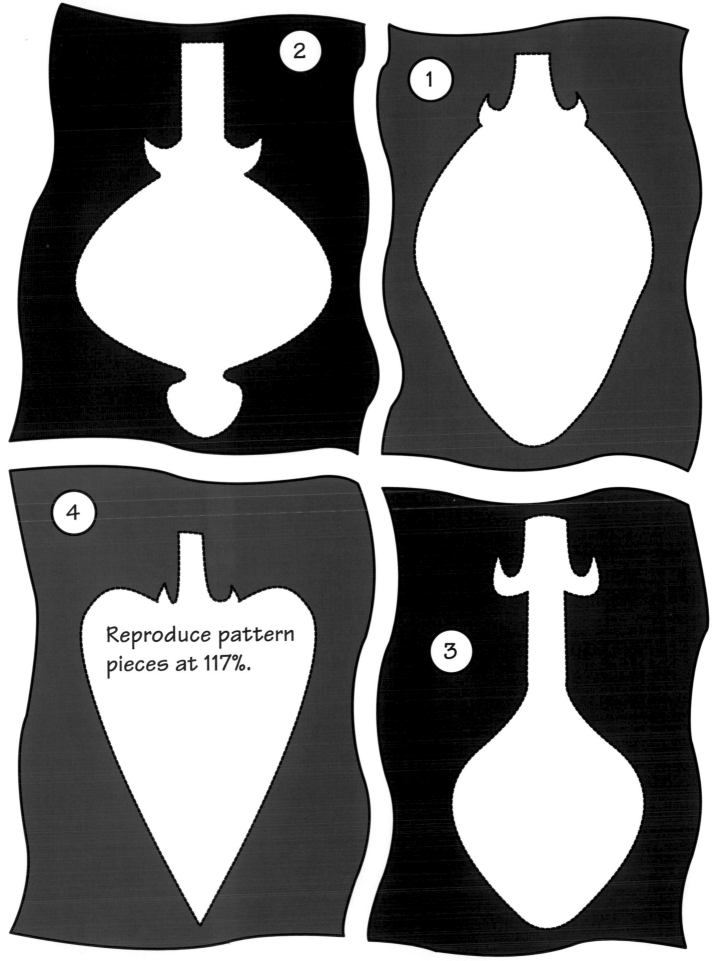

Reproduce pattern pieces at 117%.

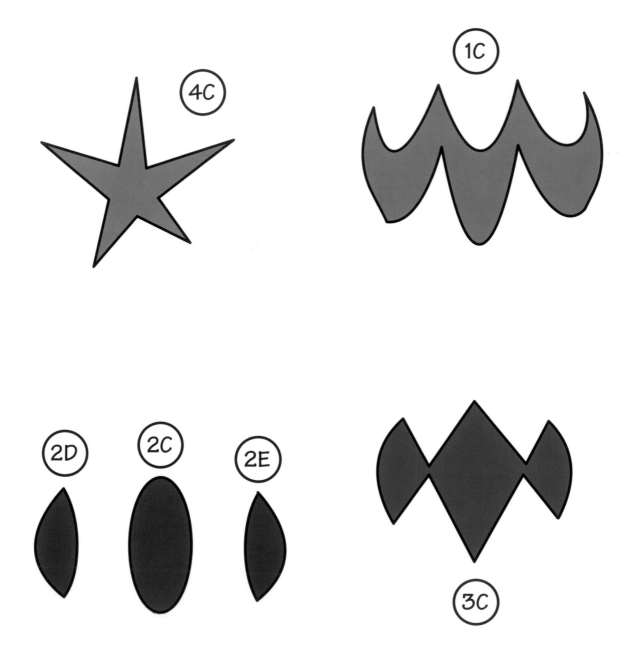

Reproduce pattern
pieces at 117%.

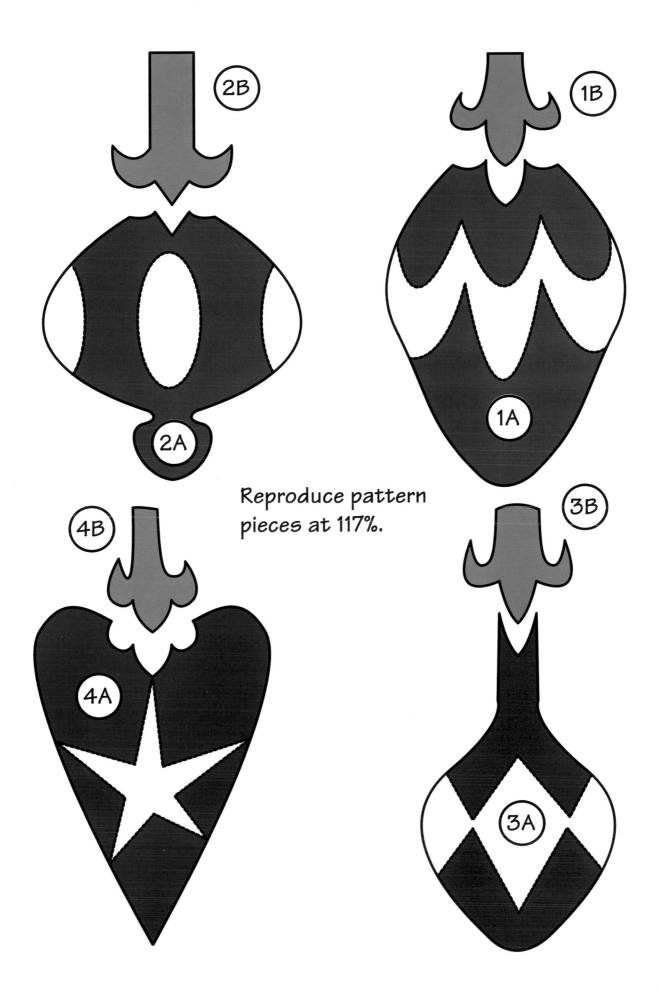

Reproduce pattern
pieces at 117%.

Santa under the stars ...

Materials

100% cotton sheeting shirt
Fusing adhesive, ³/₈ yard
Fabric writer, black
Fabric writer, gold
Pencil or non-permanent pen
Scissors
Tape measure
Straight pin
Iron
Straight pin or toothpick

Fabrics for pattern pieces

By Name	By Number/Letter	Size
Santa's Coat & Pants	1, 8	6" x 7"
Fur & Snow	2, 4, 7, 9, 11	5" x 14"
Beard	3A	3" x 4"
Face	3B	Scrap
Gloves	5	2" x 2"
Stars & Buttons	6A thru 6C, 1A	6" x 6"
Boots	10	3" x 3"

Instructions

1. Pre-wash the shirt and all the appliqué fabrics to remove sizing and reduce shrinkage. Do not use fabric softener.

2. All the patterns in this book are the reverse of how they will appear on the shirt. Lay the fusing adhesive, paper side up, onto the patterns on pages 131-133 and trace. The broken lines are positioning and/or painting lines.

3. Cut the shapes that you have traced onto the fusing adhesive apart and fuse, according to manufacturer's instructions, to the wrong sides of the appliqué fabrics. Let all fabrics cool. Do not remove paper backing yet.

4. Cut all fabric shapes out along traced pencil lines. Remove paper backing.

5. Using a pencil or non-permanent pen, transfer pattern markings and details for painting. For example: coat, snow, and facial details.

6. Find the center of the shirt by folding it in half down the center front. Press a slight crease to mark the center.

7. Measure 3" down from the neckline on the centerline of the shirt. Mark that measurement with a straight pin. This will be the position of the piece that is closest to the neckline.

8. Referring to the photograph, position the pieces on the shirt, in the following order: Santa's Coat (1), Buttons (1A), Beard (3A), Face (3B), Fur (2, 4), Gloves (5), Stars (6A, 6B, 6C), Fur (7), Pants (8), Snow (11), Fur (9), and Boots (10). Fuse all pieces at once according to manufacturer's instructions.

9. Using a gold fabric writer, outline the raw edges of all the appliqué pieces, beginning at the upper left-hand side if you are right-handed or at the upper right-hand side if you are left-handed. Continue down the front of the shirt with the gold fabric writer until you get to Santa's face. Using a black fabric writer, paint Santa's eyes. Using the gold fabric writer, finish painting the design. You may also choose to embellish with additional painted lines. Use a steady hand and constant pressure on the bottle—any stray paint splatters can easily be removed with a straight pin or toothpick.

10. Dry flat for 4 to 6 hours. The paint will cure completely in 24 hours and the shirt can be washed after 72 hours. To launder, turn the shirt inside out and wash in warm water on delicate cycle. Tumble dry on low heat.

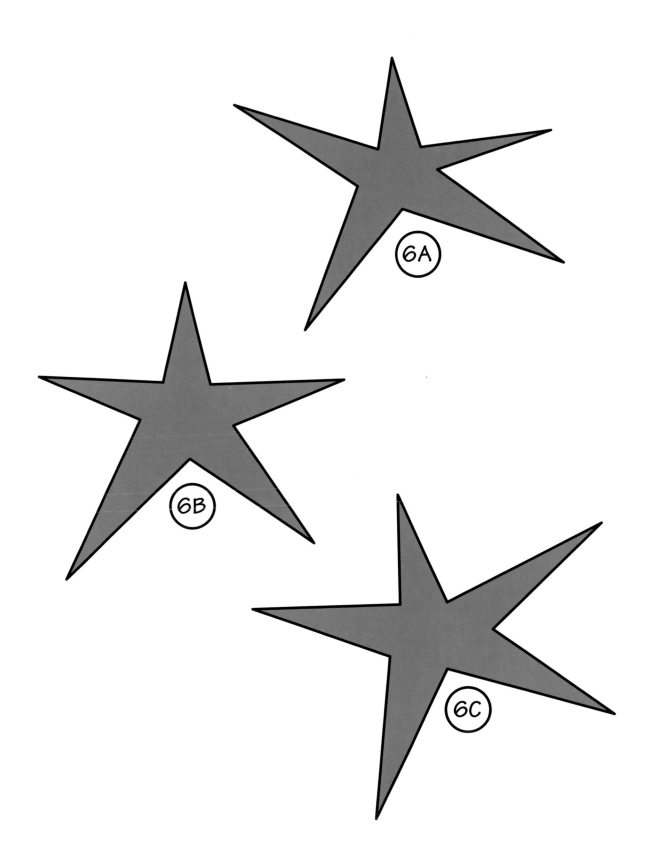

Reproduce pattern
pieces at 100%.

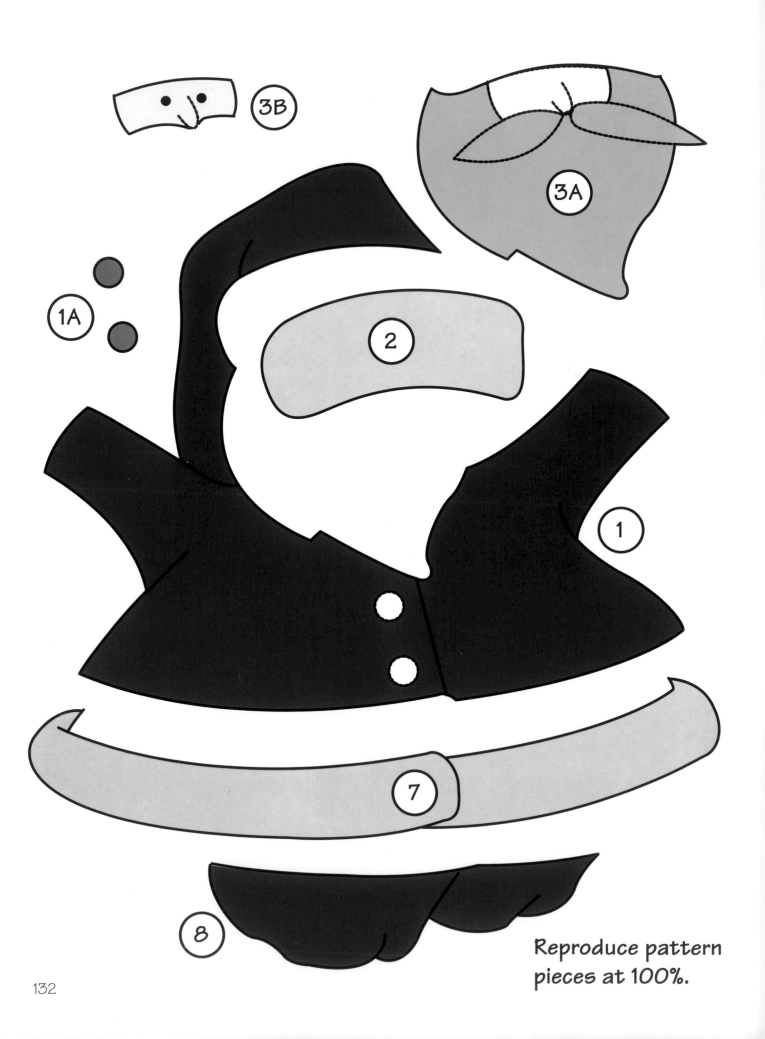

3B

3A

1A

2

1

7

8

Reproduce pattern pieces at 100%.

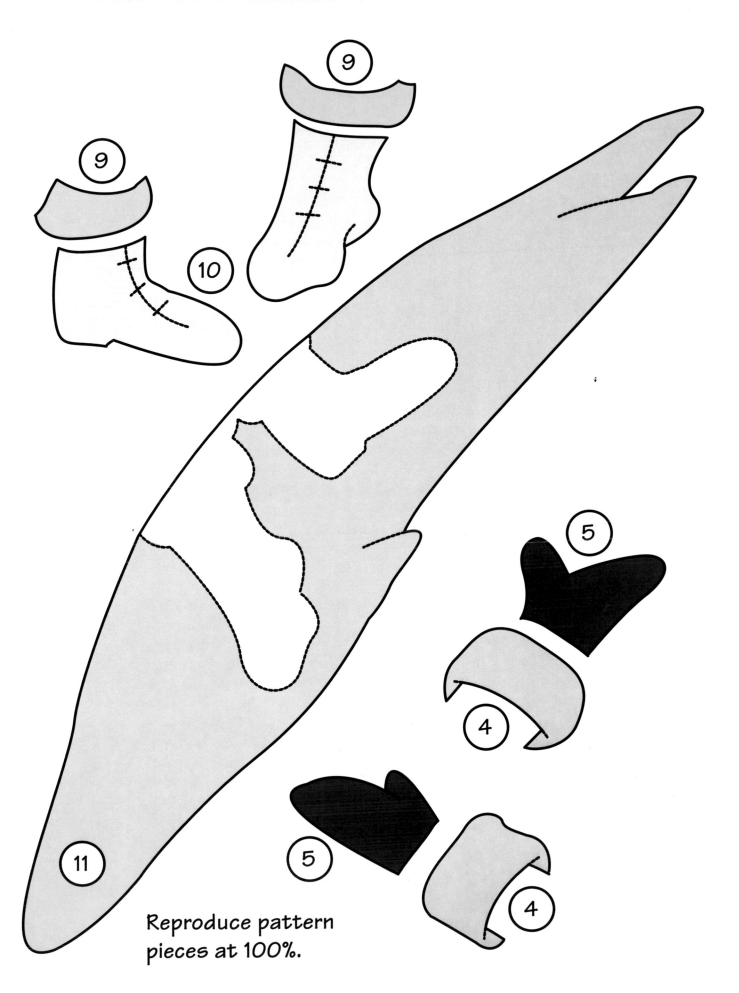

Reproduce pattern
pieces at 100%.

O Christmas tree ...

Materials

100% cotton sheeting shirt
Fusing adhesive, ³/₈ yard
Fabric writer, gold
Pencil or non-permanent pen
Scissors
Tape measure
Iron
Straight pin or toothpick

Fabrics for pattern pieces

By Name	By Number/Letter	Size
Background	1	7" x 12"
Tree	2	9" x 9"
Star	3	2" x 3"
Tree Trunk	4	2" x 4"

Instructions

1. Pre-wash the shirt and all the appliqué fabrics to remove sizing and reduce shrinkage. Do not use fabric softener.

2. All the patterns in this book are the reverse of how they will appear on the shirt. Lay the fusing adhesive, paper side up, onto the patterns from pages 136-138 (after they have been enlarged 111%) and trace. The broken lines are positioning and/or painting lines.

3. Cut the shapes that you have traced onto the fusing adhesive apart and fuse, according to manufacturer's instructions, to the wrong sides of the appliqué fabrics. Let all fabrics cool. Do not remove paper backing yet.

4. Cut all fabric shapes out along traced pencil lines. Remove paper backing.

5. Find the center of the shirt by folding it in half down the center front. Press a slight crease to mark the center.

6. Position the background (1) on the shirt front. Fold this piece in half, matching the long sides, and make a crease in the top and bottom with your fingers. Match this crease with the crease on the front of the shirt to center the design. Piece 1 should be placed about 3" down from the neckline.

Fuse piece 1 in place according to manufacturer's instructions.

7. Referring to the photograph, position the remaining pieces on the shirt, in the following order: Tree (2), Star (3), and Tree Trunk (4). Fuse all pieces at once according to manufacturer's instructions.

8. Using a gold fabric writer, paint small dots around the raw edges of all the appliqué pieces, beginning at the upper left-hand side if you are right-handed or at the upper right-hand side if you are left-handed. Make sure you leave a small space—about ¹/₈"—between each dot. If you get them too close together, they will "bleed" into each other. You may also choose to embellish with additional painted lines. Use a steady hand and constant pressure on the bottle—any stray paint splatters can easily be removed with a straight pin or toothpick.

9. Dry flat for 4 to 6 hours. The paint will cure completely in 24 hours and the shirt can be washed after 72 hours. To launder, turn the shirt inside out and wash in warm water on delicate cycle. Tumble dry on low heat.

Reproduce pattern
pieces at 111%.

Reproduce pattern
pieces at 111%.

Variations in sweatshirts ...

Turn a sweatshirt into a jacket!

Instructions

1. Turn the sweatshirt inside out.

2. Fold the sweatshirt in half.

3. Place side seams together.

4. Lightly press the fold down the center of the sweatshirt.

5. Cut one layer open along the center front fold line as shown in Diagram A.

6. To determine the amount of binding you will need (see Binding options on page 142), measure the sweatshirt from the neck to the hem and add one inch. Double this measurement to allow enough binding for both sides as shown in Diagram B.

7. If you prefer, cut the band off the bottom of the sweatshirt and bind (see Binding options on page 142).

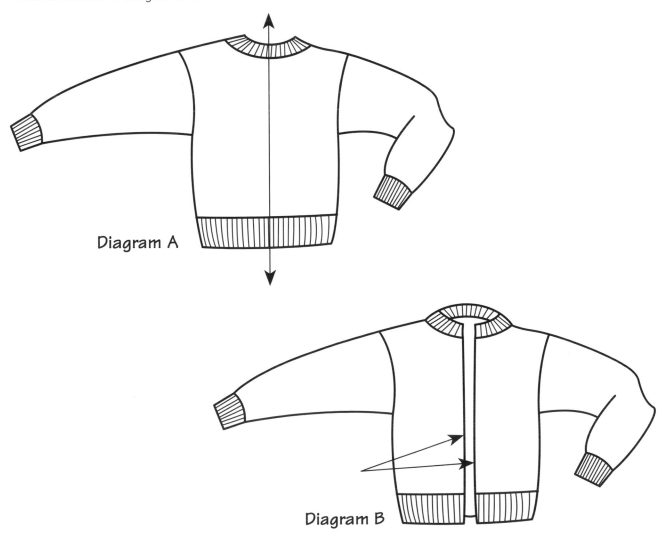

Diagram A

Diagram B

Variations in sweatshirts ...

Turn a sweatshirt into a vest!

Instructions

1. Turn the sweatshirt inside out.

2. Fold the sweatshirt in half.

3. Place side seams together.

4. Lightly press the fold down the center of the sweatshirt.

5. Cut one layer open along the center front fold line.

6. To determine the amount of binding you will need (see Binding options on page 142), measure the sweatshirt from the neck to the hem and add one inch. Double this measurement to allow enough binding for both sides.

7. Cut the sleeves off the sweatshirt as shown in Diagram A.

8. Cut the neck band off the sweatshirt.

9. Hem all cut edges or bind (see Binding options on page 142).

10. If you prefer, cut the band off the bottom of the sweatshirt and hem or bind as shown in Diagram B (see Binding options on page 142).

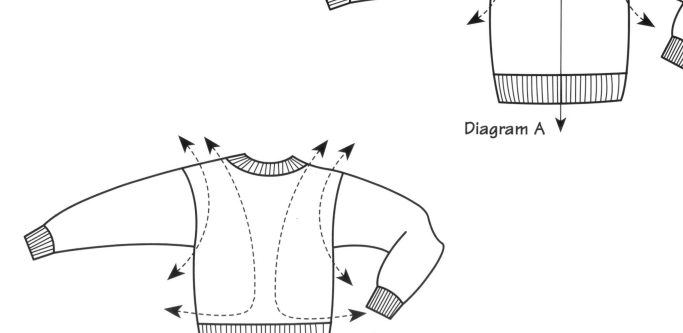

Diagram A

Diagram B

Variations in sweatshirts ...

Turn a sweatshirt into a dress!

Instructions

1. If preferred, cut the band off the bottom of the sweatshirt.

2. To determine the amount of fabric you will need for the skirt, add 3 inches to the length you want. (Purchase this amount of fabric if you are making the dress for a child and double the amount of fabric if you are making the dress for a teen or an adult.)

3. With right sides together, sew the fabric pieces together. Sew a gathering stitch along the top edge of the fabric. Gather to fit the bottom of the sweatshirt. Sew the fabric skirt to the bottom of the sweatshirt using a zigzag stitch or a serger.

4. If you prefer, you can cut the sleeves off the sweatshirt or make a V-neck. If so, hem or bind the raw edges (see Binding options on page 142).

Binding options ...

Binding with bias tape

1. Using ½" double-fold bias tape or like amount of bias tape made from the fabric of your choice, sew the bias tape to the wrong side of the fabric edge to be bound.

2. Fold the bias from the wrong side to the right side and pin in place.

3. Top-stitch the bias to the front of the sweatshirt. Tuck the ends in before finishing your stitching.

Binding with ribbon

Note: Only straight edges can be bound with ribbon. Curved edges require a bias-cut binding.

1. Using 1" satin ribbon, press the ribbon in half lengthwise. Measure and press the ends in.

2. Slip the folded ribbon over the raw edge and pin it in place.

3. Hand-stitch the ribbon to the sweatshirt on the inside and top-stitch on the outside.

Self-binding

1. Roll the raw edge 1/4" and press. Roll 1/4" again and press. Pin in place.

2. Hand-stitch the rolled edge hem in place. Use a blanket stitch around all edges to secure the hem and add a decorative touch.

3. If you prefer, use a serger to hem raw edges, then hand-stitch with a blanket stitch.

JOINING BIAS STRIPS

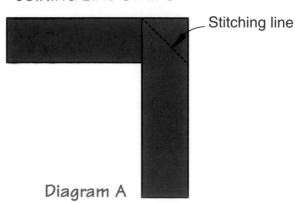

Stitching line

Diagram A

Metric conversions ...

INCHES TO MILLIMETRES AND CENTIMETRES

MM-Millimetres   CM-Centimetres

INCHES	MM	CM	INCHES	CM	INCHES	CM
$\frac{1}{8}$	3	0.9	9	22.9	30	76.2
$\frac{1}{4}$	6	0.6	10	25.4	31	78.7
$\frac{3}{8}$	10	1.0	11	27.9	32	81.3
$\frac{1}{2}$	13	1.3	12	30.5	33	83.8
$\frac{5}{8}$	16	1.6	13	33.0	34	86.4
$\frac{3}{4}$	19	1.9	14	35.6	35	88.9
$\frac{7}{8}$	22	2.2	15	38.1	36	91.4
1	25	2.5	16	40.6	37	94.0
$1\frac{1}{4}$	32	3.2	17	43.2	38	96.5
$1\frac{1}{2}$	38	3.8	18	45.7	39	99.1
$1\frac{3}{4}$	44	4.4	19	48.3	40	101.6
2	51	5.1	20	50.8	41	104.1
$2\frac{1}{2}$	64	6.4	21	53.3	42	106.7
3	76	7.6	22	55.9	43	109.2
$3\frac{1}{2}$	89	8.9	23	58.4	44	111.8
4	102	10.2	24	61.0	45	114.3
$4\frac{1}{2}$	114	11.4	25	63.5	46	116.8
5	127	12.7	26	66.0	47	119.4
6	152	15.2	27	68.6	48	121.9
7	178	17.8	28	71.1	49	124.5
8	203	20.3	29	73.7	50	127.0

YARDS TO METRES

YARDS	METRES	YARDS	METRES	YARDS	METRES	YARDS	METRES	YARDS	METRES
$\frac{1}{8}$	0.11	$2\frac{1}{8}$	1.94	$4\frac{1}{8}$	3.77	$6\frac{1}{8}$	5.60	$8\frac{1}{8}$	7.43
$\frac{1}{4}$	0.23	$2\frac{1}{4}$	2.06	$4\frac{1}{4}$	3.89	$6\frac{1}{4}$	5.72	$8\frac{1}{4}$	7.54
$\frac{3}{8}$	0.34	$2\frac{3}{8}$	2.17	$4\frac{3}{8}$	4.00	$6\frac{3}{8}$	5.83	$8\frac{3}{8}$	7.66
$\frac{1}{2}$	0.46	$2\frac{1}{2}$	2.29	$4\frac{1}{2}$	4.11	$6\frac{1}{2}$	5.94	$8\frac{1}{2}$	7.77
$\frac{5}{8}$	0.57	$2\frac{5}{8}$	2.40	$4\frac{5}{8}$	4.23	$6\frac{5}{8}$	6.06	$8\frac{5}{8}$	7.89
$\frac{3}{4}$	0.69	$2\frac{3}{4}$	2.51	$4\frac{3}{4}$	4.34	$6\frac{3}{4}$	6.17	$8\frac{3}{4}$	8.00
$\frac{7}{8}$	0.80	$2\frac{7}{8}$	2.63	$4\frac{7}{8}$	4.46	$6\frac{7}{8}$	6.29	$8\frac{7}{8}$	8.12
1	0.91	3	2.74	5	4.57	7	6.40	9	8.23
$1\frac{1}{8}$	1.03	$3\frac{1}{8}$	2.86	$5\frac{1}{8}$	4.69	$7\frac{1}{8}$	6.52	$9\frac{1}{8}$	8.34
$1\frac{1}{4}$	1.14	$3\frac{1}{4}$	2.97	$5\frac{1}{4}$	4.80	$7\frac{1}{4}$	6.63	$9\frac{1}{4}$	8.46
$1\frac{3}{8}$	1.26	$3\frac{3}{8}$	3.09	$5\frac{3}{8}$	4.91	$7\frac{3}{8}$	6.74	$9\frac{3}{8}$	8.57
$1\frac{1}{2}$	1.37	$3\frac{1}{2}$	3.20	$5\frac{1}{2}$	5.03	$7\frac{1}{2}$	6.86	$9\frac{1}{2}$	8.69
$1\frac{5}{8}$	1.49	$3\frac{5}{8}$	3.31	$5\frac{5}{8}$	5.14	$7\frac{5}{8}$	6.97	$9\frac{5}{8}$	8.80
$1\frac{3}{4}$	1.60	$3\frac{3}{4}$	3.43	$5\frac{3}{4}$	5.26	$7\frac{3}{4}$	7.09	$9\frac{3}{4}$	8.92
$1\frac{7}{8}$	1.71	$3\frac{7}{8}$	3.54	$5\frac{7}{8}$	5.37	$7\frac{7}{8}$	7.20	$9\frac{7}{8}$	9.03
2	1.83	4	3.66	6	5.49	8	7.32	10	9.14

Index ...